923
W647;

P9-CRD-062

...SSON YOUNG ADULT SERIES

I DARE NOT FAIL:
Notable African American Women Educators

MARY WILDS

KNAPP BRANCH LIBRARY
13330 CONANT
DETROIT, MI 48212
852-4283

Avisson Press, Inc
Greensboro

4/16 KN   JUN 0 7

Copyright © 2004 by Mary Wilds. All rights reserved.
For information, contact Avisson Press Inc., P.O. Box
38816, Greensboro, NC 27438 USA.

First Edition
Printed in the USA
ISBN 1-888105-64-X

Library of Congress Cataloging- in- Publication Data

Wilds, Mary, 1960—
    I dare not fail : notable African American women educators /
Mary Wilds.— 1st ed.
        p. cm. — (Avisson young adult series)
Summary: A collective biography of African American women
educators Maria Louise Baldwin, Mary McLeod Bethune,
Charlotte Hawkins Brown, Mary Ann Shadd Cary, Marva
Collins, Charlotte Forten Grimke, Lucy Craft Laney, and
Virginia Estelle Randolph.
        Includes bibliographical references and index.
        ISBN 1-888105-64-X (pbk.)
        1. African American women educators—Biography—
Juvenile literature. 2. Educators—United States—Biography
Juvenile literature. [1. Educators. 2. African Americans—
Biography. 3. Women—Biography.] I. Title. II. Series

LA2311. W55 2004
370'.92'2—dc22
[B]

                                        2003062929

Contents

Introduction:
Black Educators Who
Made A Difference

The black community's first scholars and teachers were those who learned on the sly. Slaves who lived and worked in the homes of wealthy and educated whites often taught themselves to read and write by listening in on white children's lessons. These slaves, usually women, secretly passed on their knowledge to other slaves.

When the first schools for black children opened in the 1700s black women trained as teachers by assisting white educators in the classroom. By the late 1700s black women were opening their own schools, even in states like South Carolina and Georgia where such schools were illegal. They would operate their schools in secret when necessary, and some of these "underground" schools lasted as long as 25 years.

Charlotte Forten Grimke of Philadelphia became the first black woman teacher to officially serve in the south during the Civil War. Once the war ended others educators, like Mary Ann Shadd Cary, poured into the South and Washington, D.C., hoping to do their part to educate their people. Like Grimke, most of these educators were women.

Black families had realized early on how important schooling was for a daughter. While a son could always find work as a laborer, the few good jobs open to black women usually required an education.

Cary and her fellow educators persevered despite the proliferation of Jim Crow laws in the South during the 1870s. They and their compatriots usually worked in tough conditions, living on little money and making do on their own ingenuity. Teachers in the South reported that county officials provided them a broom, a bucket and little else; thus they were forced to purchase chalk, pencils and other school supplies out of their own meager salaries. Yet educators like Lucy Craft Laney, Charlotte Hawkins Brown and Mary McLeod Bethune triumphed over these difficult circumstances while building schools from scratch. Others, like Maria Louise Baldwin blazed trails by taking leadership roles in white-dominated school districts. Baldwin, in particular, served as the first black principal in New England.

By 1901, more than 1 million black children and adults were attending school. Some teachers, like Virginia Randolph, took a practical approach to their future by focusing on "industrial" education: black students needed marketable skills just as much as they needed to learn to read and write, she felt. Others, like Brown, focused on academics: black children should be taught the same rigorous subject matter that college-bound whites learned.

But educators and students continued to struggle against segregation in schools through the 1950s. The pivotal moment came in 1957, when nine black students in Arkansas enrolled in their local high school. The governor, Orval Faubus, called out the national guard to prevent their admission. When the guard was withdrawn, white supremacists tried to block them from the school. President Eisenhower finally had to step in to protect the students. Segregation did not end that day, but by 1968, 38 percent of black students in the South attended an integrated school.

Today's black female student still faces tremendous odds. In 1997, one out of seven black girls would drop out of school before graduating. That same girl had a one-in-21 chance of being a victim of a violent crime. The odds of her becoming a doctor, on the other hand, was 891-to-one. However, modern-day black teachers like Marva Collins, still work to make the classroom a better place for their students. Collins, for her part, built a school in a modest Chicago neighborhood and went on to train other educators in her highly successful teaching methods. Thus, she and other, less-heralded counterparts around the country continue to follow in the footsteps of Bethune, Craft, Brown, and other black women educators who made a difference.

(Photo courtesy Cambridge Historical Commission)

Maria Louise Baldwin
(1856-1922)

I dare not fail.

Maria Louise Baldwin's life was, in its way, a study in contrasts. A woman considered very attractive by those who knew her, she nonetheless chose not to marry, albeit such a choice was a common one among schoolteachers of both races. A groundbreaking educator in her day, she remained a modest, self-effacing woman who did not regard her accomplishments as anything remarkable. She lived in Cambridge, Massachusetts, throughout her entire life and kept a tight circle of family and friends. Yet she mingled with some of the most famous people of her day. When she died, Maria's body lay in state for two days, so that former colleagues and students could file past and pay their respects.

Maria Louise, nicknamed Mollie by her family,

was born in Cambridge in 1856. The town of her birth is one of the oldest communities in America, founded in 1630 by a group of Puritans who'd left England in search of religious freedom. One of the oldest, and greatest, colleges in America, Harvard, was founded in the heart of Cambridge.

A small black population had lived in Cambridge from the earliest colonial days. One of its more famous black citizens was Harriet Jacobs, who ran a boarding house in Cambridge during the 1870s. She had been born a slave in North Carolina, ran away as an adult and lived in hiding for seven years before escaping to the North. Her book, *Incidents in the Life of a Slave Girl*, told of her years in bondage.

However, Maria Baldwin grew up in an ordinary home, child to ordinary parents. Her mother, Mary, originally hailed from Baltimore, Maryland. Her father, Peter L. Baldwin, was a Haitian immigrant and worked as a mailman. Maria and her younger sister attended Cambridge public schools, and in 1874, Maria graduated from Cambridge High School. Following that, she entered the Cambridge Training school for teachers and graduated in 1875.

Maria tried, and failed, to get a teaching job in

Cambridge, and so made her first and only try at living away from home. She took a job in Chestertown, Maryland, but would only spend a few years there; a group of sympathetic Cambridge residnets, knowing how much she wished to teach in her hometown, stepped in to help her. They formed a committee and collectively urged the Cambridge school board to give her a position in the public school system. In 1881, they, and Maria, succeeded. She became an elementary school teacher at the Agassiz Grammar School, located in Cambridge near the Harvard University campus. Agassiz' students were the children of Cambridge's well-established, upper and middle-class families. They were also, primarily, white.

Agassiz school was nearly a brand new school when Maria got there. Its brick and granite structure had been completed in 1875 at a cost of $25,000. It was named for Louis Agassiz, a Harvard professor who taught natural history.

Maria was 25 years old when she arrived at Agassiz school. She was fine featured, lovely, with great dark eyes, already known for her penetrating intelligence and melodious speaking voice. A voracious reader, she brought a well-stocked library into her Cambridge home. She would live quietly and carry on her work without fanfare, but even in 19th century Massachusetts, a professionally successful, intellectually sophisticated black woman could not keep a low profile. In 1889, the career of Maria Baldwin took a remarkable turn. She was named principal of Agassiz school after eight years of teaching 1st through 7th grade.

Officials in the Cambridge school system apparently made this courageous decision – hiring a black educator as principal of a white school – because Maria Baldwin was the obvious and best qualified candidate. Hallie Q. Brown, author of *Homespun Heroines and other Women of Distinction*, described the decision-making process as follows:

"Well, you know as well as I do there is only one suitable person, Miss Baldwin." said a school board member. "I think so too, but I am not sure about the color," said the superintendent. "it is not a question of color it is a question of the best."(1)

But Maria Baldwin's hiring did not happen in a vacuum. Only one year before she was born the Massachusetts legislature had desegregated all state public schools for the first time. The black community had worked for years to see that their children got the same educational opportunities that white children did.

In 1787, Black activist and educator Prince Hall lost his battle to force the Boston public school system to allow black students. Hall finally opened a school in his own home, which was located at the West Cedar Streets on Beacon Hill, which was then the heart of Boston's black community. In 1805 the school was moved from the Hall home to the African Meeting House at 8 Smith Street, the oldest black church in America. Blacks had struggled so long to get their children into public schools that Maria's appointment was a momentous occasion for her community. She would be the first black teacher in the North, and probably in the entire country, to serve as principal at a white school.

Maria was well aware of the important step she as an educator was taking and, always a modest person. "I dare not fail," she was recorded as saying. She needn't have worried, for from the first she performed magnificently.

Maria served as Agassiz' principal for 23 years. During her tenure, she established a number of innovations, organizing the first Parent-Teacher Association in Cambridge, and inspiring the beginning of a Museum of Science program in the city schools.

Concerned with the health of her pupils, Maria became the first principal in Cambridge, and possibly the United States, to establish an "open air" classroom. so that students could take their lessons out of doors. During the 19th century many people believed that fresh air and sunshine cut back on the number of colds and flu that children suffered, and so Maria ensured that her students would take at least some of their lessons outdoors. She was also the first principal in Cambridge to hire a school nurse.

Maria believed in lifelong education, not only for her staff and colleagues, but for herself. She took courses at Harvard to keep up with the latest teaching methods and taught summer courses for fellow teachers at the Hampton Institute in Virginia, and at the Institute for Colored Youth in Cheyner, Pennsylvania.

Her work and travels would allowed her to rub elbows with the likes of Booker T. Washington, black educators Lucy Craft Laney and Alice Freeman Palmer; William Monroe Trotter, publisher and editor of the Boston Guardian; Archibald Grimke, editor of the Hub newspaper; writer and historian Edward Everett Hale, and Julia Ward Howe, author of "The Battle Hymn of the Republic." Maria, a voluminous letter writer herself, treasured the correspondence her famous friends sent her.

Her role as an educator also led her to play mentor to a bright young black woman, Charlotte Hawkins Brown. Charlotte would one day found the nationally known Palmer Memorial Institute in Greensboro, North Carolina. Charlotte was born in the south, but relocated to Boston while still a girl. She obtained her education from Boston schools and went on to make her life and career in North Carolina. Charlotte would always look up to Maria Baldwin as the example of what a successful black woman could be.

"My mother's plans for me were my greatest inspiration," Brown later wrote of her role models for success. "But the position as (an administrator) in one of the select schools of the city of Cambridge held by a beautiful brown-skin woman, Maria Baldwin by name, gave great courage to my desire to forge ahead and become." (2)

Maria advised her young friend to study current events and to read noteworthy books so that she could compete with the upper middle-class white students at her school.

She also recommended she contact Alice Freeman Palmer. Palmer was a well-regarded Boston educator who helped Brown get into teachers college. Brown was so grateful she eventually named her school for Palmer.

As time went on Maria surrounded herself with a tight circle of friends and led an active life in the community. She was a founder of the Woman's Era Club of Boston and became involved in the Omar and the Banneker Club. She was also active in the League of Women for Community Service, the Boston Ethical Society and Teacher's Association.

Maria held weekly reading classes at her home for black students who attended Harvard University. One of them was W.E.B. DuBois, who later founded the National Association for the Advancement of Colored People (NAACP). In 1917, DuBois recognized his former teacher as "Man of the Month," (it was not customary to name "Women" of the month in those days) in the NAACP Journal:

"The school composed of kindergartners and eight grades is one of the best in the city and is attended by children of Harvard professors and many of the old Cambridge families ... Miss Baldwin thus, without a doubt, occupies the most distinguished position achieved by a person of Negro descent in the teaching world of America, outside cities where there are segregated schools."(3)

She gave popular lectures in Boston and elsewhere in the country on such topics as women's right to vote, poetry, and historical figures, like George Washington, Thomas Jefferson, James Madison and Abraham Lincoln. Maria "was known for her pure English and was a respected elocutionist ... She possessed a voice of remarkable sweetness and compass and had an unusual charm and manner." (4)

Maria was in her prime then, a polished and privileged woman who moved easily through society. But despite her success, she was still keenly aware of the racism that other blacks experienced. In 1915, Maria was asked to attend the Boston premier of the D.W. Griffith film, *The Birth of the Nation*. Although groundbreaking in many ways, the film was known, then and now, for its insulting portrayals of black Americans.

The events organizers asked Maria to read

poems at the opening, and to join in singing, "My Country, 'Tis of Thee." Maria did the reading but resisted singing the song, telling her hosts that many white Americans did not regard blacks as true citizens.

"Please do not sing that then," she asked the organizers, "for it would break my heart when I know the feeling of so many in Boston and throughout the country who do not truly recognize that this is our country. I might sing it another time, but not now." (5)

Maria had become an icon in the Cambridge educational community. The poet E.E. Cummings would enroll at Agassiz as a boy in 1904 because of Maria's reputation. In his book, "Six Non Lectures," he remembered her:

"Miss Baldwin, the dark lady mentioned in my first nonlecture (and a lady if ever a lady existed) was blessed with a delicious voice, charming manners and a deep understanding of children. Never did any semi-divine dictator more gracefully and easily rule a more unruly and less graceful populace. Her very presence emanated an honour and a glory … From her I marvellingly learned that the truest power is gentleness."(6)

In 1916, Agassiz school was demolished to make way for a new school. When the new one opened, the school board decided that since the school now employed 12 teachers and housed five hundred students, a school Master, rather than a principal, was needed. The position of Master was one of the highest honors an educator could receive. Maria, now Agassiz' Master, would be the only black educator in Massachusetts to be given this honor.

On January 9, 1922, Maria gave a lecture to the council of the Robert Gould Shaw House Association at Boston's Copley Plaza Hotel. She suddenly collapsed during the event and died the same day of heart disease. Clergy from several denominations participated in her funeral service, held at the Arlington Street Church. Her body lay in state for two days, so that friends, colleagues and former students might file past her caskets and pay their respects.

Tributes to Maria poured in. "Children and adults have learned from contact with Miss Baldwin a new respect and appreciation for the Negro race, whose noble possibilities her whole life exemplified," a former student said. "She has left to all whose life touched hers the memory of a rare and radiant nature, the keynote of whose character was service." (7)

The League of Women for Community Service named a library in her memory, and Cambridge Schools installed a tablet for her at Agassiz. In 1952, Howard University named one of its women's dormitories Maria Louise Baldwin Hall. In 2001, an Agassiz 8th grader, Nathaniel Vogel led a campaign to have the school renamed for its former principal.

"It seems criminal to demote a woman of her stature to a small plaque on the wall," Nathaniel said. "... Looking around my 8th grade class I saw so many different nationalities and noted that this is the kind of school Ms. Baldwin would stand for."(8)

The boy's plan had its detractors: too politically correct, some said. But Nathaniel prevailed when his campaign was picked up by the Boston Globe newspaper and local news stations. On May 21, 2002, the Cambridge School Committee unanimously agreed to change the name of Agassiz School to Maria L. Baldwin Elementary.

(Photo courtesy of the National Park Service, Mary McLeod Bethune
Council House archives)

Mary McLeod Bethune
1875-1955

*I believe, first of all, in God, and next of all, in
Mary McLeod Bethune.*

Mary McLeod Bethune's life reads like a
movie script. She was a poor sharecropper's
daughter whose education would never have gone
beyond grammar school had a benefactor not
miraculously intervened and paid for an expensive
boarding school education. She started a school
from scratch, relying on little more than her own grit
and an eye for opportunity. She hobnobbed with the
rich and powerful during the last part of her life but
never lost her concern for the poor and
underprivileged. Mary gave up a good deal to
achieve her dreams, including material comforts and
the company of her husband; she and her husband,

Alburtus, would only live together eight years in all. But these dreams, ultimately, revolved around the needs of others, rather than her own. Mary's whole life was centered on bettering the lives, and minds, of her people.

Mary McLeod was born in Mayesville, South Carolina, in 1875. Her parents, Patsy and Sam McLeod, were both slaves, working together in the cotton fields and raising children, seventeen of them in all. After the Civil War, they were freed. Sam and Patsy acquired five acres of land and built a house of their own. Mary Jane McLeod, their fifteenth child, was born there, a free little girl.

Neither Sam nor Patsy could read and write but they were more than willing to send their obviously gifted daughter Mary to school. She attended primary school in her hometown, but there was a limit to what that school could teach her. Then, when she was thirteen, Mary got a lucky break, the kind that few black girls of her era would ever see. That year, a Denver, Colorado, seamstress named Mary Crissman read of the need for education in the South. Crissman, a Quaker, took it upon herself to provide tuition for one black southern girl over the course of a year. She contacted the Presbyterian

Church, which she knew to have mission schools in the south. Would the church provide the name of a worthy candidate for her scholarship?

Church officials contacted Mary's teacher, Emma Wilson, in Mayesville, as they searched for that worthy candidate. Emma chose Mary, her best student. Sam and Patsy McLeod reluctantly bid their daughter goodbye, and even the neighbors came to the train station to see her off. Since no one in her family could read or write, Emma Wilson agreed to read Mary's letters to her family and write back to her.

Mary was on her way to Scotia Seminary in Concord, North Carolina, with only a few homemade dresses, shoes and stockings to her name. But Scotia Seminary was a good school, combining Christianity, culture and industrial education, and Mary would move heaven and earth to stay there for a full seven years. She scrounged for more scholarship money and earned the rest, working in the tobacco fields or as a laundress and cook. In seven years, she only managed two trips home. Nonetheless, she considered the separation worth it, for Mary Jane McLeod had an education. And, she had experienced kindness, in unexpected places. "I was shown goodness in my childhood," she said much later. "My parents believed in me. I learned to believe in other people."(1)

Her years at a Christian school had so strengthened her faith that Mary decided to become a missionary in Africa. She chose to prepare at the Bible Institute for Home and Foreign Missions, later known as Moody Bible Institute, in Chicago. She was 20 years old. The institute accepted her as a student but not, ultimately, as a missionary; after a year the school informed her it did not wish to send any black missionaries abroad.

"The greatest disappointment of my life," she would say of that experience. "Those were cruel days." (2)

Mary turned to the only career path open to an educated black woman at the time: teaching. She went home to Mayesville and threw herself into her new career with gusto. She even scrubbed the floors herself and greeted each student personally as he or she arrived in the morning. But Mary was only the temporary teacher in town, and when a permanent one was chosen, it would not be her. Mary went far afield to find her next job: at the Haines Industrial and Normal School in Augusta, Georgia. She also found a mentor at this school: Lucy Craft Laney, whose picture now hangs in the Georgia statehouse.

Laney had founded the school with little help and struggled for years to keep it afloat and viable. But by the time Mary arrived, Haines was a well-ordered school with an impressive library. Laney's achievement convinced Mary that education, too, would be her purpose in life. And she, too, would run her own school one day.

Mary was now 24 years old and beginning to make contacts. She met Madison C.B. Mason, the head of the Methodist Freedmen Aid and Southern Education Society. Mason raised money for black schools and recommended which schools the society should support. He would be an important resource as Mary's career progressed. One year later she left Haines to teach in another black school: the Kendall Institute in Sumter, Georgia. She met another teacher while at Sumter, one who played a very important role in her life: Alburtus Bethune, her future husband.

Mary and Alburtus got to know each other while singing in the Kendall choir. Soon they struck up a friendship and began walking home together every Wednesday after school. They married in 1900, when Mary was 25; an advanced age for a new bride in those days. Soon after their wedding the Bethunes left Kendall for new teaching jobs in Savannah, Georgia. Their son, Albert, was born there, and soon afterwards, they moved again: to start a Presbyterian mission school, in Palatka, Florida.

A mission school, however, was not her own school, and Mary had not given up on that dream. But Alburtus was happy with their situation in Palatka and would not hear of striking out on their own. Mary made the difficult decision to pursue her dreams without him. She started her own school in Palatka, but there was an area in Florida, Daytona Beach, which needed her even more.

Daytona had a burgeoning black community, and those children needed a school. One day, Mary left a note for Alburtus, packed up her books, some food, and Albert and hitchhiked to Daytona. She found an inexpensive house to rent and second hand furniture. She scavenged paper and made her own ink from elderberries. Five students showed up on the day she opened her school. A few locals gave the school food on credit and donated appliances and old furniture and dishes. Mary paid the bills by baking and selling sweet potato pies to local railroad workers. When the tourist season began she found an even wealthier benefactor: soap manufacturer

James Gamble, vacationing in Daytona Beach, patronized her sweet potato pie stand. Impressed with her gumption, Gamble donated $100 to her school.

By 1906, Mary's new school had literally worn her out. Mary's old colleague, Madison C.B. Mason, invited her to Chicago for a period of rest and recuperation. Mary accepted his invitation and became a tourist; she visited Hull House, toured Bronzeville, a Chicago neighborhood populated by southern blacks who'd emigrated to the north for jobs. Mason, head of the Methodist Episcopal Fund for Southern Education, tried to convince her to emigrate: she and Albert could stay in Chicago with him and his family and she could find a teaching job. But she declined his offer; she had a job to get back to in Florida. So go back to Florida she did – and struggled for two years. Any time she could she talked up her school, even while selling sweet potato pies in front of the town's big hotels. She took her school's little choir to sing at churches, and civic clubs. She opened her school three nights a week to adults and taught them civics, so they could learn how to register to vote.

Mary hired three other teachers at the school,

including Frances Keyser, who would become a mainstay. She also found a new site for her school – a former dumping ground on Oak Street in town. It was swampy, full of trash and mosquitoes, but available for sale. Its owner wanted more money for it than Mary could afford, but she dickered him down: $200 purchase price; five dollars down and five dollars a month. Mary didn't have the five dollars in her pocket to give him, but by the end of the day she earned it, by selling ice cream to workmen who were putting up new buildings at the beach. Some of the same men who bought her ice cream that day later drained the swamp water and burned and buried trash for her. With Albert helping she dug up ferns and wildflowers in the woods and planted them on her property.

James Gamble, the man who so liked her sweet potato pie, had built a house in Daytona Beach. In the winter of 1908, he and a group of his friends became regular contributors to her school. They formed a board of trustees and helped her find enough money to build a four-story frame building. Mary named the building Faith Hall. Three years later, in 1911, she had enough funds to put a brick building, a girls dormitory and a chapel. The school's first 8th grade class graduated that year.

Mary's school became a full-fledged high school in 1914.

Mary's missionary spirit went far beyond the needs of her school and students. Daytona Beach was in those days littered with turpentine factories; low-wage employers that hired workers with meager skills. Those who worked in turpentine factories also endured terrible living conditions. Most were illiterate and almost all of them lived out in the open, in camps. For all of her zeal, all of her social awareness, Mary had been unaware of just how bad their lives were – until the day she went on a picnic along a local river and got a look at their camps. She was furious. She returned the following Sunday, determined to treat their minds, souls and bodies. She arrived with a bible, medicine, scrubbing brushes, slates, chalk and first grade school books. She and some of the women in camp scrubbed one of the shacks clean and she led a Sunday School service. Soon she was working in four other camps; teaching school, hosting singing classes and training women and girls in home making, nursing and teaching skills.

The experience also convinced her that Daytona needed a hospital where its black citizens could get medical treatment; its current hospital was for whites only. In 1914, she and a local black doctor went before the Daytona Beach city council to ask that a ward in the local hospital be set aside for black patients. They were turned down. A few weeks later one of her own pupils was stricken with appendicitis. Mary was able to convince a white doctor at a private hospital to operate and the child recuperated at her home. Once again, Mary took matters in her own hands. She wrote her northern benefactors and in a month had the money to buy a building. Two months later, McLeod Hospital opened, with two beds in it.

In 1915, Alburtus Bethune, who was still legally married to Mary, finally came to visit her in Daytona Beach. He toured her school and hospital, and discussed their son's education. The visit, and their future relationship, was friendly, but she and Alburtus never lived together again. He returned to his latest job, teaching at a boys school in Georgia, and she continued her work in Daytona Beach, for Mary had a new cause.

American women had been demanding the right to vote since 1912. Mary joined a voting rights league, organized as part of the National

Association of Colored Women. Women were given the right to vote in 1920, but in Mary's county, it was still an uphill battle to cast a ballot, even for black *men*. Nonetheless, Mary set out to help local black men register to vote. She conducted reading and civics classes so that the women could pass literacy tests. She pushed them to pay the required poll tax despite the financial hardship it brought. About 100 in her community, men and women, qualified.

The night before the election, the Ku Klux Klan paid a visit to her school. They strode up the driveway with torches and a cross and she stood alone outside to face them. She waited, and listened, as they threatened to burn down the school.

"If you must burn my buildings, go ahead," she said. "But let me tell you. Once you've burned them I'll build them again. Then if you burn them a second time, I'll build them again and again." (3)

When they left Mary's school was still standing. The following day, she led the procession to the voting booths. News of the confrontation, and Mary's fame, spread. She would be invited to conferences and public meetings to discuss the issues of for black suffrage and black issues. She met W.E.B. Du Bois, founder of the National

Association for the Advancement of Colored People, at one conference. One of his remarks -- when he was a boy, Du Bois was not even allowed to borrow a book from his local library – stayed with her. When she returned to Daytona Beach she opened her school library to the black community. For years her library was the only free source of books for local black children.

Mary's influence was growing. Large sums of money had been donated to her school, and she had acquired more land and built a new brick dormitory for her students. Her school's curriculum included domestic sciences, nursing and music. Meanwhile, the local public schools had improved enough that she felt comfortable in dropping the lower grades and concentrating on high school and college courses.

In 1923, her school merged with the Cookman Institute, located in Jacksonville, Florida. This new enterprise, Bethune-Cookman College, was operated by the Methodist Education Board, which named Mary Bethune-Cookman's president. A remarkable achievement for a sharecropper's daughter – yet Mary's friends believed she needed a respite from achievement for a while. They surprised her with a generous gift, an eight-week, all-expenses-paid trip to Europe, in 1923. She accepted the gift, left her beloved school behind and spent weeks as an honored guest on the continent. She had an audience with Pope Pius XII, and dinner with the Lord Mayor of London. And upon her return from Europe, she made a new friend, one who would change her life. While in New York, she was invited to lunch at the home of Sara Roosevelt. Sara was the mother of Franklin Delano Roosevelt, a rising New York politician whose career had stalled after a bout with polio. She met Franklin's shy and brilliant wife, Eleanor, at the luncheon. The two became friends.

She was now president of a college, friend to the famous and soon-to-be famous, but Mary McLeod Bethune was not yet ready to rest. Back home in Florida, she made a very public announcement: the state still had no public high schools for black children and it was a disgrace. Too few blacks, she said, were willing to speak out. She understood that most of her people still lived in shanty towns and were intimidated by the Klan. Still, they couldn't let fear rule their lives, she said.

"If we have the courage and tenacity of our forebears who stood firmly like a rock against the lashings to slavery and the disruptions of Reconstruction," said Mary, "We shall find a way to do for our day what they did for theirs."(4)

Determined to make life better for her people, Mary became president of the Southeastern Federation, a group of clubs that agitated for better housing and jobs for blacks. Her hopes were high and were quickly dashed by forces outside her control. The Great Depression had arrived with the Stock Market Crash in 1929, and the black community, never affluent to begin with, was hard-hit.

Bethune-Cookman College remained open and retained its teaching staff, but only because Mary worked without a paycheck: she took no salary so that her teachers could be paid. She would use every bit of her legendary resourcefulness to keep her students in school and the hungry locals who showed up at her door fed. In 1932, as people all around her suffered, she was named one of the fifty greatest women in American history by a popular magazine. The honor must not have been a comfort to her; too much injustice and suffering still existed in the world. The jobless rate among southern blacks alone was 69 percent. And when food and aid were handed out to the needy, blacks had to wait in line for leftovers; whites were always taken care of first. Mary protested angrily at the unfairness of it all.

"They admit the patient is sick with fever," she said. " They admit that the he is hungry and needs to be fed: because he is a Negro, they suggest that half a meal will suffice." (5)

Mary supported Franklin Roosevelt, husband of her friend Eleanor, for president in the 1932. One year later, Roosevelt asked her to come to Washington. He appointed her to the advisory board for the Black Affairs Director of National Youth Administration. Her supervisor on this project would be future President Lyndon Baines Johnson.

From the beginning Mary agitated for more blacks to become involved in the process of finding jobs and opportunities for her people. "It does not matter how equipped your white supervision might be, or your white leadership, it is impossible for you to enter as sympathetically and understandingly into the program of the Negro, as the Negro can do," she reasoned. (6)

While living in Washington, Mary took a small apartment in one of the few buildings that would rent to blacks – like many southern cities, Washington was still segregated. Two years after she joined the board Mary was awarded the Springarn Medal, given annually to the Black American who had made the greatest contribution during the year.

During her work for the National Youth Administration she consulted with church leaders, lawyers, doctors, labor and teachers, and Eleanor Roosevelt herself in her quest to search out opportunities. Through Mary's efforts, and the efforts of many others the National Youth Administration put thousands of young people between the ages of sixteen and twenty-four to work. These young people worked in libraries, public offices and farms; built roads, dairy barns, schools and playgrounds. Financial assistance from the Youth Administration helped more than 40,000 young people attain their college degrees. Despite all this success, Mary still felt frustrated. Not enough was being done for southern black children, she felt. They deserved a better shot at an education.

In 1934 she went to see Roosevelt with her concerns and was promptly named the Director of Minority Affairs. She immediately set to work on making a new batch of dreams come true.

By 1936, Mary was setting up schools around the rural south. Thanks to her, more than a million southern black children finally got the rudiments of an education. Mary also created vocational training programs: agriculture, shop work, and sewing. Those who participated in her programs were paid while they learned.

Mary was now an elderly lady and her health was failing. Still, she continued to travel, giving hundreds of speeches each year. By 1942, she was ready to return to her home on the Bethune-Cookman campus; however, her country and people needed her again. War had broken out with Germany and Japan, and Americans black and white rushed to support their country's cause. So many black women were volunteering for the Women's Army Corps that a black person was needed in the War Department to oversee the placement of these women. Roosevelt called on Mary again, and she accepted his challenge. She officially resigned from Bethune-Cookman College to become special civilian assistant in the War Department, and in 1945, when the war ended, the NAACP sent her to a conference to observe as the charter for the United Nations was hammered out.

She retired at long last, in 1950. But her health was failing and retirement was short: Mary died on May 18, 1955. She had lived long enough to hear the United States Supreme Court declare, in 1954, that segregation was unconstitutional.

(Courtesy of the N.C. Office of Archives and History)

Charlotte Hawkins Brown
1883-1961

If staying in his place (means) jimcrow cars, segregated districts ... doing all the menial tasks, the handing out of the back door of some restaurant a sandwich ... the Negro today will never find his place.

Charlotte Hawkins Brown married twice but only had one child: her school, the Palmer Memorial Institute in Sedalia, North Carolina. Charlotte built a school from scratch, following in the footsteps of such pioneer educators as Lucy Craft Laney, who believed that education paved the path to equality. Charlotte tied herself emotionally and financially to her school: she spent as much time raising money as she did teaching and the constant strain of keeping her school open and afloat finally ruined her health. The Palmer Memorial Institute could not go on without her, and it eventually closed after she died. Yet its grounds and buildings are kept as a memorial to the woman who worked so hard for so many, and devoted her life to a personal vision of what her people could become.

Charlotte Hawkins Brown was born in Henderson, North Carolina in 1883. Her mother was Caroline Hawkins, daughter of ex-slaves and an unmarried woman. Charlotte would grow up without her natural father, who would never be identified, either by her mother, her family or Charlotte herself.

Caroline and Charlotte moved to Boston, a town already known for its liberalism and tolerance, when Charlotte was five years old. Caroline got married one year later, to a man named Nelson Willis. Caroline and Nelson ran a business together, taking boarders and operating a laundry out of their home. Charlotte grew up comfortably, in a community fairly free of prejudice. She took advantage of the many educational and cultural opportunities Boston offered her, learning to play the piano, finishing primary school in less than three years and attending the local high school.

" (I) knew nothing of segregation," she said

much later. "There were for me no barriers of which I was conscious. I went where I wanted to go, sat where I wanted to sit, and had scores of intimate friends, young and old, in both races."(1)

By participating in the Union Baptist Church in Cambridge Charlotte met many local and national black activists who came to speak at the church: Booker T. Washington, W.E.B. DuBois, Lucy Craft Laney. In 1897, when she was 16, Charlotte attended a speech given by Washington, "The Negro in the South," which made a strong impression on her.

By this time, Charlotte had already decided to become a teacher. While still attending high school, she met the two women who would help her achieve those goals. Charlotte had an after-school job as a babysitter and would often study and care for the baby at the same time, pushing its carriage along with one hand and carrying her schoolbook in the other. This passer-by was Alice Freeman Palmer, the white president of Wellesley College and a member of the Board of Education for the state of Massachusetts.

Realizing just who she'd met, she was, and mindful of her own plans to be an educator, Brown wrote to Palmer, explaining that she'd been the girl behind the baby carriage. Palmer remembered her and offered to pay some of the expenses Brown would later incur at school. Brown did indeed study education at a two-year state school, but she did not formally graduate as planned. Instead, she followed another course set for her by a woman she met by chance.

The woman, whom she met on a train, was secretary to the American Missionary Association (AMA). The AMA operated schools for blacks in the south, which in those days insisted on separate schools for blacks and white students. Thanks to her new acquaintance, the AMA offered Charlotte a teaching job at the Bethany Institute in Sedalia, North Carolina. Charlotte arranged to finish the last of her education classes by mail and in the fall of 1901, at the age of 18, she traveled by train to Sedalia.

Sedalia was a tiny town with no electricity, no telephones and no public library. Charlotte found her new students eager and polite but reading and writing at far below their grade levels. Many of them had to walk 10 miles or more to school. Charlotte tried to lessen the burden on her students, at least the female ones, by turning an old blacksmith's shop across the street from the school into a girls' dormitory. She did her best, but after only one year after she arrived, the Bethany Institute closed. The AMA, strapped for cash, could no longer afford to keep it open. Charlotte could have gone home to Boston, but she had found a cause in Sedalia and would stay, despite the racial prejudice of local whites and suspicions of black residents, who questioned her motives for staying. Charlotte, only 19 years old, was determined to open her own school in Bethany's place.

Charlotte went back to Boston temporarily and looked up her old mentor, Alice Freeman Palmer. Running a school required money and she hoped Palmer would help her find it. She was not disappointed; Palmer sent many donors her way, and the money came pouring in, despite Palmer's sudden and untimely death. Back in Sedalia, the grieving Charlotte renamed her one-year-old, one-room school the Palmer Memorial Institute in 1903.

Charlotte wore many hats from the very beginning. She was chief fund raiser, educator, surrogate parent and visionary. In three years, Charlotte's vision was succeeding: she built her first new building, Memorial Hall, complete with classrooms, offices, library, kitchen and dining area, in 1905. Palmer's first three graduates graduated that same year. By the end of 1907, Charlotte was overseeing a staff of five, including herself and two former students. She built a new boys dormitory, opened a student-run farm at the school, and continued fund raising. Always ahead of her time, Charlotte also set up a nursery and kindergarten for the children of local working mothers.

Her community outreach continued. She opened a community clinic at the school and sponsored meetings so that local farmers could consult with the school's farm expert. But in 1909, when she was 26 years old, Charlotte's personal life caught fire. She had gone home to Boston to visiting her mother and stepfather when she met and fell in love with one of their boarders, Edward Brown. Edward was a Harvard student and 10 years older than Charlotte. Charlotte remained in North Carolina while carrying on her romance with Edward, and in 1911, two years later, the pair were married. Edward joined his new bride to Sedalia and Palmer Memorial Institute but, apparently, he never felt at home there. He and Charlotte would separate after only one year of marriage. It remains a matter of speculation as to what went wrong in their relationship. Edward may have been disappointed by the small-town atmosphere and lack of career opportunities. Or, Charlotte's single-minded commitment to her school and dream could have been too much for him– and for her. But for whatever the reason their marriage was over. They divorced in 1916, though Charlotte would carry her former husband's name for the rest of her life.

By 1910, Charlotte's "child" had grown up. Palmer was an 80-acre campus that offered classes in carpentry, mechanics, cooking, sewing, house keeping, agriculture, and sex education (a radical concept for the early 20th century). Six years later, Palmer's 55 alumni included more than 15 teachers and two high school principals, as well as those who'd gone on to study religion and medicine. In 1917, Palmer Memorial Institute celebrated its 15th year and seemingly, all was well. But then, without warning, fire broke out on campus. The industrial building and its adjacent commissary burned and because Sedalia had no fire department, students, teachers, residents and Charlotte herself were forced to battle the blaze alone, with little more than a bucket brigade to aid them.

All in all, the school suffered $7,000 in losses, including a larder of food. But this time, local benefactors stepped in. White businessmen in nearby Greensboro came forward with a pledge of money and support.

"I have never seen people more touched than the Greensboro people," Charlotte said. "I feel that my calamity has brought a condition that nothing else would produce."(2) She repaid their kindness with a performance by the Sedalia Singers, the Palmer Institute's singing group. The group performed in Greensboro in January, 1918, and as a special concession to Charlotte, the performance was opened to blacks and whites. Ordinarily, Greensboro audiences would have been segregated.

This goodwill between Charlotte and the Greensboro community thrived at a time when the Ku Klux Klan numbered 100,000 strong in the South. The year after Charlotte's Sedalia Singers performed in Greensboro, over 70 southern blacks were lynched. Several of these victims were soldiers in uniform, returning home after serving their country in World War I. It was a frightening time for an outspoken black woman, but Charlotte was not easily frightened. She would one day tell the story of how, while on a train trip to Memphis, she settled down for the night in a berth in the "white" sleeping car. She was awakened that night by a group of angry white men who ordered her to either move to the black car or face being put out at the next station, where, they said, a lynch mob waited. Charlotte was forced to walk through three "whites-only" cars to get to the "blacks-only" car. She was at the time on her way to address the Woman's Missionary Association, a group of white women who defied convention by inviting black speakers to address their meetings. Some of the women she marched past on the train were white women en route to the same meeting.

Charlotte sued the railroad and won a settlement, but her nature was more one of reconciliation than confrontation. In 1919, she had published her first book, *Mammy*, a short novel meant to win the sympathies of southern whites by harkening back to the "good old days." Her novel, based on a true story, told of a former slave and her husband who honored a promise to their master to stay with his family until he came home from the Civil War. He never returned, of course, and the couple stayed with the white family until the end of their days, despite their own children's pleas to come north.

Charlotte may have hoped to arouse fond memories and feelings among southern whites who read the book, but it received mixed reviews among her own people and white friends. And soon, Charlotte found herself going far beyond the writing of a sentimental book to reach equality. By 1926 she had given speeches on race relations at such venues as Berea College in Kentucky. Too much needed to be done and too few white southerners lacked respect for blacks as thinking people, she said. As for Palmer Memorial Institute, it was shifting its focus to becoming the kind of place that produced "thinking" black people. No more would Charlotte simply offer courses in industrial education and domestic science. Her students would also study English, mathematics, civics and science. Those who wished could take classes in Latin, physics, chemistry and French.

Palmer Memorial Institute in the 1920s was a place for learning and practicality. It was also a new home for a handsome young teacher named John William Moses. John was well-dressed, dapper, and 15 years younger than Charlotte. She fell in love and married him in 1923. Not long after the wedding the new groom suddenly announced he would take a business trip to South America. He was part-owner of a diamond mine there, he explained to his bride, and he had to sail immediately. Charlotte bid him goodbye but then decided to travel to New York to meet his returning ship. But he was not on it. John, in fact, was nowhere to be found. After some digging, Charlotte learned the truth. There was no diamond mine, no business, and in fact John had actually gone to New York to be with another woman. Charlotte returned to North Carolina without him, and had her marriage annulled. Never again would she try marriage. She would focus all her efforts on her school and put down some deep, permanent roots right on the school's campus. She built a home for herself, Canary Cottage, near central campus. Single or not, she would not let life slow her down, keeping a busy social life at Canary Cottage and hosting many visitors, including her brother's children, whom she helped care for.

Palmer Memorial Institute celebrated its 25th anniversary in 1927. The school was flourishing but Charlotte herself was going downhill. Many years of hard work, constant fund raising and travel, and the break-up of her second marriage had wreaked havoc on her health. The year her school celebrated its silver anniversary Charlotte finally took a leave of absence. Thanks to some generous benefactors – she had a little money of her own—Charlotte was able to sail to Europe on an extended tour. Upon her return she found herself in great demand as a speaker. Making full use of her well-polished speaking skills and dignified demeanor, Charlotte was a powerful force for change, arguing that blacks and whites deserved the same educational opportunities.

Meanwhile, back at Palmer, she expanded the educational opportunities for her own students. A two-year junior college was added to the Palmer campus in 1928. Her students were now also able to study voice and piano, dramatics, orchestra, art and public speaking, and participate in sports. But when the Great Depression sucker-punched the local economy, contributions began to dry up. She was forced to take out a mortgage to help pay expenses and in 1932, lost another building to fire. Worst of all, the 1930s saw the loss of her most faithful backer, the AMA.

The AMA's decision to withdraw its support nearly cost her her school and career but Charlotte was able to convince the AMA to stand by her for one more year while she reorganized the board and made other arrangements. Palmer survived, but with its budget severely cut. Charlotte would have to increase her fund raising efforts even more, at a considerable cost to her own health.

Palmer lost its day students when a public

school for black students finally opened in the area, so the school turned its attention to its boarding community. Despite the budget cuts, Palmer's students studied religion, the fine arts and organized sports teams and clubs. With other black boarding schools around the country closing their doors, Palmer nearly stood alone in the kind of education it could offer to young blacks. Her students enjoyed literary societies, proms, recitals, Friday night socials – all the educational experiences that would stand them well in society. Charlotte indeed saw herself as turning out the kind of young person who would fit in easily in the upper classes. To that end, she published a book on manners and etiquette, *The Correct Thing to do – to Say – to Wear* in 1941.

The book and its subject matter sound hopelessly old fashioned today, but for decades *The Correct Thing to Do* was required reading for decades at black colleges and universities.

"Don't save your table manners until company comes," Charlotte wrote. "You and your family are just as good and deserve just as much consideration as any of your friends and acquaintances."(3)

At this point in her life Charlotte believed firmly that black youths needed more than just book learning to get along in the world. In order to compete with whites, they would need the same cultural know-how and etiquette training that whites received from a very young age.

Charlotte was by this time mindful of her poor health, and the fact that Palmer would need someone to guide it after she was gone. She began a lobbying campaign to convince the state to include Palmer in the state university system. In 1940, the governor rejected her proposal that Palmer become a state college—and countered with a more insulting suggestion. Why not make Palmer into a home for black delinquent girls instead? Charlotte firmly rejected that idea.

She decided on a new strategy: fiscal restraint. By 1943 the school was free of debt and Charlotte was building an endowment. Meanwhile, Palmer's reputation grew and by the end of the 1940s, more than 1,000 students were applying annually for Palmer's 30 vacancies. They were the children of wealthy and upper middle class black families and their attention, and that of their parents, got Palmer a featured spot in Ebony Magazine in 1947.

But five years later, in 1952, Charlotte was a 69-year-old woman in poor health who could no longer keep up with the demands of running a school. She decided to retire and asked a Palmer instructor, Wilhelmina Crosson, to take over as Palmer's president. She stepped down in October of 1952 while keeping the title of director of finance and Canary Cottage. She had run Palmer for fifty years and had difficulty letting go. Even worse, she began to lose her memory.

Her behavior became erratic: she would visit a class, and if something happened that she didn't like, she would interrupt the class, dismiss the student and order them to the chapel so she could lecture them.

In 1956, the Palmer board asked Charlotte to leave campus and sever her ties with Palmer, for the good of everyone. She refused and her bad behavior continued. In 1958, the board held an emergency meeting. Charlotte attended, interrupted frequently and angrily, and the board voted to remove her from campus. Charlotte's niece arrived on campus to look after her, and after a medical examination, she was declared incompetent. Eventually, she was placed in the home of a former employee, where she could be attended by a nurse around the clock. Charlotte died in 1961, of complications from diabetes.

It may have been too much to ask that Palmer continue long without Charlotte, its founder and driving force. Crosson's successor, Harold Bragg, was such a poor administrator that his decisions sent the school into financial ruin. Burdened by debt and strapped for cash, the Palmer campus was sold in 1971. But the state of North Carolina honored Charlotte sixteen years later when the Charlotte Hawkins Brown Memorial State historic site was opened and dedicated in 1987. The site is now open to the public, but Charlotte's legacy goes far beyond what visitors can see: hundreds of former Palmer students who went on to study medicine, teaching and other professional endeavors.

(National Archives of Canada / C-29977)

Mary Ann Shadd Cary
1823-1893

We should do more and talk less.

Mary Ann Shadd Cary crammed many lives into her 70 years. She was an educator, journalist, newspaper editor, Union Army recruiter, attorney, wife and mother. She was also an early starter, having begun to teach school while she was still a child herself. Mary Ann was an American woman who spent much of her adult life in a foreign country—Canada— and a black activist who was usually at odds with the American black establishment. She probably faced as much discrimination as a woman during her lifetime as she did as a black American. She was the first black woman to edit a newspaper, she endured insults from those who deemed such work "unseemly." She was probably the first black woman ever to attend law school, and the school may have delayed awarding her diploma because she was a woman.

Mary Ann had a prickly personality and never backed down from a fight: she probably made as many enemies as she did friends. But if one thing could be said about Mary Ann Shadd Cary, it was that she was never afraid to try anything. If she wanted to do something, she did it.

Mary Ann Shadd was born in Delaware in 1823. Her father, Abraham Shadd, a shoemaker, was an early supporter of civil rights and equal education. In 1833, when Mary Ann was ten, her family moved to Westchester, Pennsylvania, one of the largest black communities in the north. Westchester, about 15 miles south of Philadelphia, was a community of farms and mills, of free blacks and abolitionists. It was also home to stops on the Underground Railroad. Southern Pennsylvania had more underground railroad routes than any other northern state. Escaped slaves would make their way north on this "railroad" by staying in safe houses maintained by abolitionists, sympathetic whites and free blacks. One of those free blacks was Abraham Shadd. His farm was located on a northern branch of the railroad coming out of Washington, D.C.

Abraham has been identified as one of three blacks in Westchester who helped a prominent Quaker bookseller-Quakers were firm abolitionists-guide runaway slaves through the region.

But Abraham and Harriet had come to Pennsylvania for the sake of their children; not the underground railroad. Back in Delaware, their children were not allowed to go to school: state law forbid the teaching of blacks, who were also excluded from some churches. The Quakers, who strongly believed in education for all, ran schools for black children in Pennsylvania. Mary attended one of these schools in Westchester. Her Quaker education would have included religion, philosophy, literature, writing, math, Latin and French, and exposed her to Quaker values of brotherhood among people of all races. While still in her teens Mary launched her own career as a schoolteacher, working in Norristown, Pennsylvania and Trenton, New Jersey. She was also showing signs of political activism, not to mention having a mind of her own. She wrote to the newspaper run by celebrated black activist Frederick Douglass', the North Star, criticizing blacks' penchant to gather and talk, but not act.

"We have been holding conventions for years,"

she wrote, "Have been assembling together and whining over our difficulties and afflictions, passing resolutions on resolutions to any extent; but it does really seem that we have made but little progress considering our rhetoric."(1)

In 1851, Mary went to take a job in an all-black school in New York City. Despite its bustle and energy, New York City was as segregated a place as anyplace else in the United States. Mary Ann Shadd, with her stiff-necked independence, made quite an impression on New York's black community. Black activist William J. Watkins related this anecdote about her. It became part of local legend. It seems that Mary Ann had wanted to hail a horse-drawn cab despite her color.

In New York and coming down Broadway at a time when colored women scarcely dared to think of riding in the (cab), Miss Shadd threw up her head, gave one look and a wave of her hand. There was such an air of impressive command in it that the huge, coarse, ruffianly driver, who had been known to refuse colored ladies as though suddenly seized with paralysis, reined up to the curb, and she entered, and without hindrance, rode to the end of her journey.(2)

But Mary Ann's sojourn in New York would be brief, due to events that occurred beyond her control, namely the Fugitive Slave Act of 1850. The act was meant to lessen the strife between abolitionists and slave owners, and between the North and South, but ultimately it made the situation worse. The new law allowed individuals who could prove ownership of a slave to seize that slave in a northern city. It also levied stiff penalties on those who harbored runaway slaves.

This turn of events encouraged more American blacks to move to Canada, though the trend had been ongoing since the Revolutionary War. Slavery had never taken hold in Canada because its early economy was based on the fur trade, not plantations. Only a few Canadian families employed black servants and white loyalists who moved to Canada during the American Revolution usually freed their slaves after they arrived. After 1833, blacks in Canada were awarded the same rights as whites. Canadian blacks could vote, serve on juries and own property.

I Dare Not Fail

After the Fugitive Slave Act, thousands of blacks sought freedom in Canada. One of them was Mary Ann Shadd.

Mary Ann attended an anti-slavery conference in Toronto in 1851 and met many prominent Canadian blacks, including Henry Bibb, founder of the first Canadian black newspaper, *Voice of the Fugitive*.

"I have been here more than a week, and like Canada," she told her brother, Isaac. Canadian territory west of Toronto was also in dire need of teachers. Mary Ann opened a one-room school in Windsor, and charged her students one shilling a week, a steep price for those days. Despite the promises touted by black Canadians, life north of the border was no paradise. Mary Ann's new town was the most destitute black community she had ever seen. In order to keep her school open she could not pay herself a salary. Instead, she depended on charity and money her parents sent to buy food and pay rent.

Mary Ann taught students ranging in age from four to 33, and some of those students were white. Living conditions were harsh: bouts of cholera and measles ran rampant through the community, and her school lacked books and basic supplies. Somehow Mary Ann managed to teach history, botany, grammar, arithmetic and geography all the same.

Her efforts did not go unnoticed. Local missionary, Alexander McArthur wrote of her in glowing terms. "Miss S. is a young (light-colored) lady of fine diction, refined address, and Christian deportment: and possessing an energy of character and enlargement of views well-fitting her for the work of teaching amongst such a people as this."(3)

She operated her school from 1851-1852, with help from McArthur, the *Voice of the Fugitive*, and the American Missionary Association, which sent her $125 a year. Despite the hardships Mary Ann embraced her new Canadian home with fervor. In June, 1852, nine months after she arrived she published a 44-page essay on Canadian immigration. Saddled with a lengthy title, *A Plea for Emigration, or Notes from Canada West*, her essay downplayed the bad aspects of Canadian life. Part travel guide, part promotional brochure, Mary Ann wrote of good soil, cheap land, jobs in the timber industry. She also extolled Canada as a place free of prejudice. Here, however, Mary Ann whitewashed the truth. Racial prejudice and segregation existed in Canada, in ample quantities. Still, Mary Ann had become convinced that Canada was the best hope for her people. Blacks in America shouldn't sit and wait for slavery to end; they should move to Canada instead.

In March, 1853, Mary Ann shut down her school; she had no more money to run it. But she had new financing, new backing, and a new plan for a newspaper. She and two backers, Samuel Ward and her friend Alexander McArthur, published the first issue of the *Provincial Freeman* on March 24, the day after her school closed. The *Freeman*'s debut turned Mary Ann Shadd into North America's first black woman editor. The following month she traveled to Philadelphia to promoting her favorite cause: black emigration to Canada. She was all of 29 years old.

In the fall of 1853, she and her supporters moved the *Provincial Freeman* from Windsor to Toronto. The newspaper published weekly from an office on King Street in Toronto and circulated as far south as Detroit, Pittsburgh and Cincinnati.

Mary Ann published articles on black issues and women's rights; boys and girls should both have an equal chance at a good education, she declared. She gave a forum to women writers at a time there weren't many. However, having a woman *editor* was simply too much for most readers. Most disagreed with the notion of having a woman at the helm, and said so. For the sake of appearances Mary Ann relinquished the editorship to William P. Newman, a Baptist minister. But she was still the paper's driving force behind the scenes.. The *Provincial Freeman* reflected her views, attacking slavery, criticizing the politics of all-black settlements, and soliciting funds to help runaway slaves. In 1855, Mary Ann moved the paper again, to Chatham, Ontario.

Chatham was a thriving community of 10 churches, six schools, numerous mills, shops, foundries, stores and farmland. It was also a important stop on the underground railroad. Mary Ann was probably hoping for more advertising and financial support in Chatham, but the *Freeman* struggled to stay afloat. It had many readers but few advertisers, and neither had the cash to pay their bills. Mary Ann often had to accept livestock, bread, cheese, or wood in lieu of money. She continued her speaking tours as a way to pay bills and support the cause of black emigration. In 1855, she was the sole Canadian delegate at the Colored National Convention in Philadelphia. She was also one of only two women in the conference. Mary Ann gave a forceful speech on Canadian emigration that observers said rocked the convention hall. The speech made her into a minor celebrity, but by then she had already left Philadelphia to tour the United States for paid speaking engagements and to speak out against slavery. She was often heckled and insulted as she traveled, particularly since she encouraged slaves to runaway to Canada.

But in 1856, these travels stopped, albeit briefly. On January 3, she married Thomas F. Cary at her sister Amelia's home in St. Catharines, Ontario. She was 32 and her new husband was 30. Thomas was born an American but had emigrated to Canada in the 1850s. He ran a barbershop and an ice business in Toronto and was a vocal opponent of slavery.

Thomas was also a widower with three young children. Little is known of his courtship of Mary Ann, and why, after such single-minded devotion to her career, she decided to marry a younger man with children. The answer might be that Thomas simply understood her in a way that other men didn't. From the beginning of their marriage the two maintained separate homes, highly unusual for that era. Thomas stayed in Toronto, she lived in Chatham and they took turns visiting each other. Mary took care of the paper and he his own business interests but despite this hard work, they knew financial hardship throughout their marriage. Toronto was in the throes of a financial recession at this time, and Thomas' shop and ice business struggled. At one point he had to sell oil lamps on the streets to get by. His financial troubles may have kept him from seeing Mary Ann as often as he'd have liked. Their long separations led to such longing missives as this one: "(write) a long letter (so) that I will get in on Sunday morning and it will be food for me on that day as I keep in my shelf all of that day."(4)

The year she got married Mary Ann transferred formal ownership of the paper to her brother Isaac and a business group. One year later, she gave birth to a daughter, Sarah Elizabeth. The new mother still occupied a prominent place in the Canadian black hierarchy, so much so that when white antislavery activist John Brown traveled to Canada in 1858, he met with Mary Ann.

Three years later Brown and his sons had been in Kansas to take part in a struggle between abolitionists and slavery supporters. Abolitionists had already been murdered in Lawrence, Kansas; on May 24, 1856, the Browns killed five slavery supporters at Pottawatomie Creek. The murders had turned Brown into a national celebrity.

By the time Mary Ann met him, Brown had formulated a plan to free America's slaves by force. His trip to Canada was actually an attempt to recruit supporters for the armed revolt he planned. Although only men were wanted for his army, he did gain aid and support from Mary Ann. She had never advocated violent overthrow of the government herself, but apparently she felt Brown's plan was good enough to support. One of her Canadian friends, Osborne P. Anderson, accompanied Brown back to the United States. Anderson was with Brown in Harpers Ferry, Virginia, where on October 16, 1859, his army seized a United States arsenal and armory. A company of United States marines led by Robert E. Lee captured Brown and his company, though Anderson was able to escape. He made his way back to Canada, and Mary Ann published his account of the battle, *Voice from Harper's Ferry*. John Brown was tried for treason and murder and hanged in Charlestown, Virginia.

"Had she been a man, she probably would have been with John Brown at Harper's Ferry," William Wells Brown wrote of Mary Ann.(5) But Mary Ann was not a man, and besides, she had more pressing problems close to home. After seven years in business the *Provincial Freeman* shut down, too overburdened by debt to continue. And in 1860, Thomas Cary died, apparently of overwork, at the age of 35. Mary Ann was pregnant with their second child, a boy, Linton, and she had been married for less than five years. She was a young widow, jobless, cut adrift with children to support. She thrashed about for something to do, applying for a West African teaching job with the American Missionary Association. But the job didn't pan out. Tired of relying on her parents for financial support, Mary Ann joined her sister-in-law, Amelia Freeman Shadd, at the elementary school Shadd founded in Chatham, Ontario. Mary Ann put her fund raising skills to work for Amelia's venture. As usual, she dreamed big: she and Amelia would open a high school some day in Chatham, she hoped..

The Civil War had begun in America but Mary Ann regarded it all as a distant event, having little to do with her and her family. She had been married to a Canadian man and had borne Canadian children. She'd run a Canadian newspaper and raised money for Canadian schools. America could be left to its own struggles. But in 1863, her attitude changed.

I Dare Not Fail

After Gettysburg and Vicksburg, Lincoln called for half a million volunteers to shore up the Union's military strength. Union General John Andrews was authorized to raise the army's first black regiment. Andrews asked abolitionist George Stearns to help him, and he in turn appealed to activists like Frederick Douglass and Martin Delany. Delany wrote to Secretary of War Edwin Stanton with a plea: the army needed more black recruiting agents. In December, 1863, he turned instead to an old friend: Mary Ann Shadd Cary.

If Mary Ann would personally recruit black soldiers for the Union Army, she would be paid up to $15 per recruit. Moreover, the position would be temporary so she could keep her home in Chatham, and continue raising money for Amelia's school in her spare time.

Leaving her children in her family's care, Mary Ann crossed the border alone. From the very beginning she was excited about her recruiting plans, despite the dangers involved. Mary Ann's territory was the Midwest, a difficult place for any black person to be. Writes Mary Ann's biographer, Jane Rhodes, "In the 1860s (the Midwest) was an especially daunting – and even dangerous – task for any black person. The Midwest was a bastion of white supremacy second only to the South, and was the site of discrimination laws, race riots, and anti-black activities, including threats, intimidation and violence."(6)

But Mary Ann pressed on, refusing to be intimidated. She went to black churches, pubs and even street corners to find recruits. After a year of constant travel, Mary Ann went home, happy to see her family again. But life was not the same in Canada, particularly after the war ended. Despite Mary Ann's fund raising efforts, her sister-in-law Amelia was forced to close the school. Many of Mary Ann's friends, colleagues and relatives were abandoning Canada, hoping to make a new life in America now that slavery had ended. Mary Ann herself was reluctant to leave, but her job prospects in Canada were nil. In 1867, Mary Ann moved to Detroit, Michigan, a progressive city where blacks could vote and attend school. She was 45 years old at the time but willing nonetheless to start over. She settled on Woodbridge Street, a predominantly black neighborhood, and obtained her Michigan teacher's certificate, but in the end she would not stay. Washington, D.C., in those times was *the* place to be for free blacks and ex-slaves. During the 1860s alone, the city's black population jumped from 60,000 to 100,000. Abraham, Mary Ann's brother, moved to Washington in 1870, and niece Mattie would follow. Absolom Shadd, Mary Ann's uncle, had operated a successful Washington restaurant and hotel in the 1830s and Isaac Cary, her husband's brother, owned a barbershop in the city. Between 1807 and 1861 more than 60 black schools were opened in Washington, making for plenty of career opportunities. In 1871, Mary Ann took a teaching job in Washington and left the Midwest.

Mary Ann's children, Sarah and Linton, moved to Washington with her. Despite her long absences they remained a close family. Mary Ann was an anomaly of her generation in that from the beginning of her marriage she had been a working wife and then a working mother. Women of her day simply did not mix career and motherhood. Once again, Mary Ann moved against the grain. As a young widow, she had of course been forced to eke out some sustenance for her family; yet, even if her husband had lived, Mary Ann more than likely would have continued in her career. Her mixing of career and motherhood, though unconventional for its time, appears not to have affected her relationship with her children. Sarah, Linton and Mary Ann would live together in one way or another throughout their lives.

By 1873, Mary Ann had been named principal of Lincoln Mission School, one of Washington's more prominent black private schools. It had been founded as an industrial school by the American Missionary Association but within two years had evolved into a thriving night school for adults, located at Second and C streets in Washington proper. Mary Ann supervised 25 teachers and staffers and oversaw 150-200 students, most of them adult blacks who wanted to better themselves, during her first year. Her teachers, many of whom were younger than their own students, taught reading, writing, arithmetic, geography, grammar and sewing. Mary Ann worked in the Washington, D.C., school system for more than a decade, but soon, teaching was no longer enough of a challenge for her. She wanted a new career. She wanted to be a lawyer.

In 1869, Howard University accepted students for its first law class ever. One of them was Mary Ann, 46 years old and the only woman in the class. She was apparently the first American black woman to enroll in law school and one of the first American women of any color to pursue the legal profession.

However ground-breaking her actions might have been, actually completing degree requirements and earning a diploma proved extremely difficult. Mary Ann worked while going to school and had to be an educator by day and a law student at night. Her brother, Abraham, also enrolled at Howard Law School and completed the program ahead of her. He went on to pass the bar in Arkansas and Mississippi and went on to establish a successful law practice in Mississippi. But Mary Ann, burdened by hard work and the need to earn a living, struggled to complete her classes. Some sources have also suggested the university was reluctant to present her for graduation because of her sex and her age – thus her law studies extended well into her 50s.

Not surprisingly, her health suffered. But despite numerous illnesses, financial problems and a heavy school workload, she remained active politically. Mary Ann found the time to became a spokeswoman for women's voting rights. In 1871, she actually tried to register to vote, only to be rejected by a board of registrars that included two black men. Mary Ann even argued before the

Judiciary Committee of the United States House of Representatives that, under the fourteenth and fifteenth amendments, women had a right to vote.

Now entering the last decade of her life, Mary Ann was still a powerful and articulate spokeswoman for her people. Yet her difficult life showed itself in her frequent remarks; she often despaired of black people ever bettering themselves. She criticized her people, opining that blacks lacked unity, and that they were unable or unwilling to learn from the past. And the living conditions for blacks in Washington, D.C., no doubt exacerbated her pessimism. Blacks in the city were routinely arrested and beaten by the police. Jobs were scarce and poverty rampant. She must have indeed wondered, how much progress, after all these years, black people had really made.

"Thousands of colored men and women are whipped and murdered in the south, and sneers and incredulity meet one on every hand," she wrote.(7)

But she did meet her personal goal, obtaining a law degree, in 1883. She was 60 years old at this time and retired from teaching. She added the word "Esquire," to her name to make it clear to everyone that she was now a lawyer. She advertised a law practice in the business section of the city directory, but despite her best efforts, actually putting her law degree to work was problematic. The Washington, D.C., Bar Association did not admit blacks or allow them to use its law library; this made work as a fulltime lawyer difficult if not impossible. Thus, most blacks ran their law practices in their spare time while working fulltime jobs.

Mary Ann made a go of it, but could not earn a living during the last 10 years of her life. So she lived with one or another of her children, depending on them financially. Both of her children had done well: Linton had worked as a messenger in the United States House of Representatives while still in his teens. Sarah was a school teacher until about 1885, when she left the teaching profession and opened her own dressmaking business. In 1892, like his father before him, Linton Cary died suddenly at a young age, 32. The death of her only son must have broken her heart and spirit. Mary Ann died of stomach cancer a few months later, at the age of 70. Her estate was valued at only $150, and her most prized possessions were her books. Her surviving child, Sarah Cary Evans, wrote a fond and tender essay about her mother for Hallie Quinn Brown's 1926 book, *Homespun Heroines.*

Mary Ann went on to become a folk hero in Canada. The city of Toronto dedicated a public school in her honor, and her life and career are studied in history and women's history classes in Canada. Her essays and articles are included in Canadian anthologies and Canadian folksinger Faith Nolan wrote a song about her.

Marva Collins has always been a staunch advocate of education—reading, writing, and arithmetic. Here she shows "Donahue" television talk show host Phil Donahue one of the basic readers used at her West Side Preparatory school in Chicago. 1982 photograph. (AP/Wide World Photos)

Marva Collins
1936 --

All you really need for teaching is a blackboard, books and a pair of legs that will last through the day.

Marva Collins spent much of her career dealing with one controversy or another. During her stint as a public school teacher in Chicago, her already fractious relationship with administration and her fellow teachers erupted into open warfare when she defied her principal's last minute order to not to go on the field trip that she'd promised her students. She went anyway, but her boss' punishment was enough to make her quit public education for good.

Determined to educate children in a manner she found most effective, Marva opened a private school, Westside Preparatory, on the second floor of the building she and her husband owned. In just a few years, this modest venture achieved celebrity status, as would its creator. Marva was profiled on the popular newsmagazine program "60 Minutes" and her life story was made into a movie starring Cicely Tyson. But the praise turned into criticism when a barrage of articles and television reports dismissed her success as a "carefully constructed media hoax that was aimed at "crippling public education (in Chicago) and around the country."(1)

But Westside Preparatory School stayed open nonetheless, and its founder stayed her course. Marva unapologetically promoted her ideas and methods and by 1999, two new schools, bearing her name and using her teaching methods, opened in Milwaukee and Cincinnati.

Marva Knight Collins was born in Monroeville, Alabama, in 1936. Her father was Henry Knight, one of the richest men in Monroeville. Marva would describe her childhood as full and wonderful, though isolating. She was the only child in town, white or black, with her own horse. Marva wore pretty, ruffled dresses to her segregated school, where she sat next to children who picked cotton and wore 25-pound flour sacks in lieu of dresses. Marva got so tired of being different from her classmates that she begged to be allowed to go pick cotton with them. Her parents finally relented but changed their minds when she came home with a bad cold after only two days in the fields. Instead, Marva went to work in her father's store, helping him count receipts and roll coins.

Henry Knight's grocery store had once belonged to his father. He parlayed the financial assets he'd inherited into a string of enterprises, including a cattle ranch and a funeral parlor.

Marva spent much of her free time with her father. He treated her more like a son than a daughter, taking her on cattle-buying trips when she was only seven years old. It was on these trips that she learned some of the hard truths of racism. The day would come when her father's hardnosed business sense got him in trouble. He outbid some buyers from big Alabama meat-packing houses who were vying for the cattle he wanted. After the sale, these buyers backed Henry into a corner. He'd cheated them, they said, and shouldn't show his face again at a sale. But he stood his ground, insisting he'd made a fair bid and would be back, no matter what they said. Finally, other buyers at the sale broke up the fight and Marva and her father were able to leave. When Marva's mother learned what had happened she tried to convince her husband to stop going to cattle sales. He refused, declaring, "I'm not going to stay away, I can't die but once."

Even when cattle sales were peaceful, the Knights still felt the burden of their race. Black cattle buyers like Henry Knight were forced to sit separate from whites. They had to use separate drinking fountains and restroom. Yet, life in the segregated south still had its joys, as Marva remembered years later. She spent her days collecting pine cones in the forest, playing on the low, red-clay hills, sliding down mud banks and wading in creeks. She usually spent her evenings reading books: bible stories, Nancy Drew mysteries, works by noted black educator Booker T. Washington. When Marva was nine years old her aunt Ruby introduced her to Shakespeare. "I asked if I could borrow (MacBeth)," Marva said. "While I was not able to grasp its full meaning I was fascinated by the action and characters of the play."(2) But Shakespeare was not taught in her local elementary school. The little school, with is unpainted walls and wood-burning stove, was for black children only and therefore, got the educational leftovers. But Marva took what learning she could, from home and from school, and in the fourth grade she met a teacher she would never forget. This teacher had a wholly different approach to learning: she praised her students, she helped them.

"Children need immediate feedback," Marva said years later, when discussing her own teaching philosophy. "I do not wait for days before returning papers. Errors mean nothing to a child several days later when the class has moved on to something else."(3)

Marva's girlhood and early education came to an end when she graduated from grammar school and went on to high school. Black high schools in 1950s Alabama were known as training schools. "I suppose it was white folks' way of saying that all black women would never be anything more than homemakers and domestics," Marva would later comment, drily.(4)

Girls at black training schools were expected to take home economics, but when the time came Marva signed up for typing instead. The school principal tried to force her to take Home Ec on her but backed off when she told him she already knew all she would ever need to know about housekeeping.

Marva graduated, without a Home Ec credit,

and went on to Clark College, an all-black liberal arts college for girls. Her father paid her way even though everyone he knew told him he was wasting his time and money educating a girl. Marva graduated from Clark in 1957; she was the first person in her family ever to go to college. She'd earned a degree in secretarial science but took a teaching job at Monroe County Training School, because it was one of the few jobs open to her.

Marva taught typing, shorthand, bookkeeping and business law courses to 10th, 11th and 12th graders. It was a good job but she was 23 years old and ready to strike out on her own. While visiting her cousin in Chicago, Marva impulsively applied for a secretarial job. She also met her cousin's neighbor, a man named Clarence Collins.

Clarence was one of 11 children and already a devoted family man. Neighborhood children followed him everywhere and a few of them even tagged along when he took Marva on their first date. His patience with, and love for, children impressed her. Within a year she became his wife.

The young couple moved into a graystone, two-flat house in Garfield Park. Their first son, Patrick, was born a year later. They had another son, Eric, three years l ater, and Marva went back into teaching, at Delano Elementary School. She found it a constructive, energizing experience at first. The principal at the school read Homer's *The Iliad* to children during their lunch period. Other teachers took Marva under their wing and encouraged her to get creative with her teaching.

But over the years, the culture in her workplace, and in the Chicago Public School system, began to change, Marva said. To her mind, too many teachers lacked passion for their craft. Rules, standardized tests and milk money collection were more important to them than teaching. Collins also championed phonics, a teaching technique that had fallen out of favor in her school. (Phonics gets children reading by having them learn vowel and consonant sounds first.) Her dissatisfaction with the status quo alienated her from her peers.

Then came the conflict with her new principal. She had planned a field trip to reward her students for their accomplishments: her principal said he had not given permission for it, she said he had. She left school with her class and other teachers, hearing of the conflict, sided with the principal. Rumors began to circulate: Marva beat her students, she wrote their papers for them. Marva considered quitting but couldn't, her family needed her income. Clarence was working two jobs already, and the added financial strain was unfair to him, she decided. Besides, she wasn't ready to leave the students in her class.

Marva tried to relax during Christmas break so she could go back to school refreshed and ready to teach. But a bombshell awaited her when she returned to work. The principal called her into his office and broke the news: he was taking her class away from her. One of the school's longtime teachers was retiring, he explained. He wanted to make her last few months at work as easy as possible so was giving her Marva's students. Marva would teach a different group of students. Once again, she considered quitting. But some unexpected allies, her students' parents, came to her rescue. They gathered angrily in the principal's office and threatened a boycott if Marva had to leave her classroom. The principal relented. He reinstated Marva with her students, but still, she had had enough. At the end of the year, she quit her job and never looked back.

Marva was now a thirty-nine-year-old woman starting over. But she wouldn't have to wonder what to do with herself for long. In July 1975, a group of Garfield Park parents approached her with a question: would she help them start a school in their neighborhood? In September of that same year, Marva and the parents opened Daniel Hale Williams Westside Preparatory School on the campus of Daniel Hale Williams University. Marva was the new school's director. She oversaw five students, including her own daughter, Cynthia. She was also a staff of one, teaching the class as well as running the school.

By January of 1976, her class had tripled in size, helped along by a television segment and an article in the *Chicago Defender* newspaper. For many of those students, Daniel Williams was a last resort. Many of those who came to her had behavioral or academic problems. Marva had no illusions as to how and why they'd come to her classroom. "Most of the parents knew very little about me or the school," she said. "They came because we had an open door and empty desks. I was just one more alternative to be tried."(5)

Marva saw herself as an innovative teacher who used tried-and-true methods to help her kids succeed. Westside's students, once labeled slow learners and failures, were given challenging authors to read: Edgar Allen Poe and O'Henry.

I Dare Not Fail

By the end of May, 1976, every one of Marva's students had improved their reading and math skills. That summer, the parents who'd helped organize Daniel Williams asked her if she would like to run it herself. She accepted their offer and renamed the school Westside Preparatory. Since the university space where she'd been holding classes was no longer available, she and Clarence went on a hunt for rental space. They searched all over Garfield Park but in every instance, either the rent was too high or the landlord didn't like the idea of having a school on his property.

In the end, they decided to stay close to home: they would open Westside Prep in the vacant second-floor apartment in their building. Clarence remodeled the space for her and a friend donated desks and blackboards. Westside Preparatory School opened with 18 students, including her son Patrick, in September, 1976. Thirty desks had been crammed into the small apartment, and school books, paperbacks and hardcovers, were stacked everywhere.

From the beginning Marva ran a strict classroom. "I told the girls not to walk around with their socks falling down like a scrubwoman's or with their nail polish chipped," she said. "Everyone knew there would be no gum chewing, nail biting, unbuttoned shirts, loose shirt tails, jazzy walks, jive talk or finger snapping."(6)

She also took some very controversial stances that would get her in trouble later on. For example, Marva opposed the notion of black history and a separate "black" culture. "I think it's foolish and hypocritical that many people allow black youths to take on extreme styles and mannerisms under the guise of finding their black identity – without pointing out the social and economic consequences," she would say. "I encouraged them to become universal people, citizens of the world."(7)

And in order to be a citizen of the world, one had to read the literature of the world. Marva's kids read Aristotle, Chaucer, Louisa May Alcott, Shakespeare and Maya Angelou. Marva tried hard to concentrate on teaching them great literature and mathematic skills and not to worry about the financial struggles of running a school; maintaining such focus was tricky, however. Income from tuition barely covered operating expenses. Only half the students paid the required $70 per month. Some paid only what they could afford, and others paid nothing. Marva had already cashed in her $5,000

Chicago schoolteacher's pension, and that money had already been eaten up by start-up costs associated with opening up Westside. Clarence managed to help pay the bills by taking on part-time construction and carpentry jobs on the side.

Then in the spring of 1977, Westside's fortunes took a dramatic turn for the better. Marva had read an article in the *Chicago Sun-Times* newspaper declaring that high school students in the Chicago suburbs never read Shakespeare, didn't know where he had lived, what he had written or even who he was. Figuring a little publicity would be a big boost for the school and for her kids' egos, Marva wrote that columnist, Zay Smith, and told him of all the Shakespeare her students read. Smith dropped by the school and was astonished by what he saw. Second graders stood up and recited passages from Shakespeare, Longfellow and Kipling for him. Third graders talked about Tolstoy, Sophocles and Chaucer. He wrote about the school and included essays written by the students, on Michelangelo, Da Vinci and Hinduism, in his story. Smith's column was also picked up by news service and published elsewhere in the country.

Suddenly, financial contributions, and letters, came pouring in. In 1978, *Time* magazine published a story on Marva and Westside Preparatory. Marva appeared on the television news programs, *Good Morning, America,* and *Sixty Minutes.* Movie producers paid her $75,000 for her life story. Westside was finally able to move out of the crowded apartment and into the old, and vacant, National Bank of Commerce building, located only a few blocks away. In September, 1980, Westside Preparatory School had enrolled 200 students. Five hundred more were on the waiting list.

Marva had taken her kids for tests at a private school the previous year and found that their math, vocabulary, spelling and reading skills had improved enormously. The administrator at that school told her her children were scoring higher and making greater progress than any other group he tested.

Marva added new staff to go along with Westside's new space. Her school was now drawing students from all over the city and from the suburbs. It was also drawing criticism. Some were offended by Marva's controversial opinions and others claimed that Marva had hand-picked the brightest students she could find just to make her test scores look good. She also drew fire for admitting white students. But Westside continued to grow, and in

September, 1981, barely a year after her last move, Marva found another, larger facility: two adjoining one-story brick office buildings on the outskirts of Garfield Park.

Meanwhile, controversy continued to brew. The president of the United Federation of Teachers and former colleagues at Delano levied serious charges at her. They said that she exaggerated her results, fixed her pupils' test scores, and raised her school's average test scores by getting rid of kids who did not perform well.

A movie based on Marva's life and work starring Cicely Tyson aired on television in December, 1981. Soon afterwards, Marva's critics struck back. A newspaper published by an organization of substitute teachers ran a story alleging that Marva's kids were not underachievers as she claimed, but middle class children handpicked by Marva for their academic ability. Other media jumped on the bandwagon. Stories critical of Marva and Westside ran in the *New York Times*, *Wall Street Journal* and *Washington Post*. An article in *Newsweek* magazine stated that while Marva had decried the use of federal aid by educators she herself had accepted $69,000 in CETA funds from 1975 to 1979. Marva answered those charges by declaring she had no idea that money had come from the federal government. The same article also stated that Marva had refused to let some of her students off the school bus because their parents were late with their $150 monthly tuition. Other parents were quoted as saying that Marva had misrepresented her credentials, mistreated students and would not release test scores for verification.

Marva went on the television talk show hosted by Phil Donahue to answer her critics. Back home, Westside parents and community supporters held rallies for her. And her school remained open and continued to grow. By the mid-1980s, Marva was giving speeches on education and commanding fees of up to $10,000. She was also drawing support from Hollywood and the music world. Rock star Prince became co-founder and honorary chairman of the Marva Collins National Teacher's Training Institute and donated money from his Purple Rain album to the institute. Former "A-Team" TV star Mr. T stepped forward to sponsor 60 students from Chicago's tough Cabrini-Green public housing project.

One of the educators Marva trained in her methods opened The Marva Collins Preparatory School, in Cincinnati in 1990. A second school was opened in Milwaukee a few years later. And in 1995, *60 Minutes* correspondent Morley Safer returned to Chicago and to Westside to interview 33 of her original students.

During the segment Safer pointed out some sobering statistics. By now, at least one member of the Westside group should have been murdered, he said, two should have been in prison and five should on welfare. But none of that was true. Marva's former students had gone on to college, graduate or law school, started their own businesses or found good jobs.

"I'm convinced," Safer said, "That Marva Collins is one hell of a teacher."

Charlotte Forten Grimke
1837-1914

"Had my first regular teaching experience, and to you and you only friend beloved, will I acknowledge that it was not a very pleasant one."

Charlotte Forten (Grimke) in some ways is the tragic figure of the story of the black women who went south" hoping to do good for their people, writes Nancy Hoffman in her essay on Charlotte's life. "(Charlotte) went south expecting to find herself in a community that would welcome her and feel very familiar. "To her great surprise, she discovered she had more in common with white, educated women in the south than she had (with) freed slaves." (1)

Today, Charlotte Forten Grimke is better known as an intellectual, author and diarist than as an educator. Nonetheless, Charlotte performed one very important task that sets her apart: she was the first black, northern schoolteacher to teach former slaves in the south. The experience might have turned her off from teaching for good, so disillusioned was she with post-slavery black culture and so out-of-place did she feel in the south. But Charlotte Forten Grimke was an idealist, and idealists are more often disappointed by life than pleased. And her childhood, within a family filled with idealists, did little to prepare her for those disappointments.

Charlotte was born in Philadelphia in 1837, into an important and influential family that occupied the very uppercrust of black society. Her father, James, was a free black who'd first made his mark as powder boy for the Continental Army. James later became a wealthy, and well-regarded, sailmaker, who by the 1830s saw his personal fortune grow to $100,000. He was hardly alone in the upper rungs of Philadelphia's black community, however. Slavery had ended early in Philadelphia, around 1800, and blacks had poured into the city ever since. By 1840, 10,000 free blacks were living in Philadelphia, and their community mirrored that of the whites: they had their poor, middle class and elite. Charlotte and her family definitely belonged to the elite. Philadelphia's upper-class blacks were educated, skilled and rich. Some were also known for their snobbery. Other less fortunate residents complained that the wealthy blacks failed to muster their resources for the common good of the black community.

James Forten, however, was not one of those blacks. He would donate a considerable amount of his fortune to the anti-slavery movement. His grand house was always open to runaway slaves and abolitionists who needed a place to stay. The woman he married, also named Charlotte, was an active member of the Philadelphia Female Anti-Slavery Society. His sisters, Margaretta, Harriet and Sarah, became minor celebrities in their day. Margaretta opened her own grammar school and offered long years of service to the anti-slavery society. Harriet started a sewing school for underprivileged girls and later in life, supported women's rights and racial desegregation. Sarah, a writer, penned many poems and essays on slavery.

Life for the Forten family was comfortable and interesting: they counted among their friends the famous Quaker poet John Greenleaf Whittier. But life for any black in Philadelphia could also be dangerous. The larger the city's black community, the more racial tensions grew. Race riots and anti-black violence erupted even as Charlotte was growing up.

Plus Philadelphia's schools were segregated, and the Fortens wanted better for their daughter. Charlotte attended school in Salem, Massachusetts, and completed her education there. The school system eventually hired her, and she would be its first black teacher. She was also the first black educator ever to teach white children in Salem. But Charlotte expected more of herself, and like her father and mother, was every inch the abolitionist. So at the age of 25, in the middle of the Civil War, Charlotte accepted an offer from noted white abolitionist and educator Laura M. Town to teach newly-freed slaves in St. Helena, South Carolina.

She may have been the first teacher, but Charlotte was following in the footsteps of other black women who wanted to help the Union cause. Harriet Tubman is perhaps the most famous of these freedom fighters, working as a spy for the Union Army. Another Union supporter, Susie King, worked as a laundress and nurse for the 54th Massachusetts infantry. Mary Todd Lincoln's personal servant, Elizabeth Keckley, was black, and the great Sojourner Truth collected food for black soldiers in Michigan. Mary Ann Shadd Cary, at great risk to her own safety, recruited soldiers for the Union Army in the Midwest.

Like the others, Charlotte went at her new duties with high hopes. But all good intentions aside, Charlotte was unprepared for the changes that awaited her. She immediately tried to embrace the local culture, but found instead that it made her lonely for home. She described the depressing effect that a musical performance by local children had on her: "The effect of the singing has been to make me feel a little sad and lonely tonight," she said. "A yearning for congenial companionship will sometimes come over me in the few leisure moments I have in the house. ... Kindness ... I meet with constantly but congeniality I find not at all in this house."(2)

She found her new charges eager to learn but difficult to deal with. "The first day at school was rather trying," she would write. "Most of my children were very small and consequently restless. Some were too young to learn the alphabet. ... But after several days of positive, though not severe treatment, was brought of out of chaos, and I found but little difficulty in managing and quieting the tiniest and most restless spirits. I never before saw children so eager to learn."(3)

I Dare Not Fail

Charlotte's work in South Carolina was actually quite controversial. It was known as the Port Royal Experiment and supported by black activist W.E.B. Du Bois, one of Town's friends. He would be the first scholar to highlight their contributions and give them their due. Other observers, however, were not so kind. Wilbur Cash, a Southern journalist and writer, dismissed the project and its teachers. They were, he said, "busybodies: they were horsefaced bespectacled old women (Charlotte was in her 20s at the time) who went where they had no business and inflamed the passions of southern whites in the process."(4)

But scholar Jacqueline Jones, writing of Charlotte and colleagues, sees them as idealists whose efforts sometimes took a wrong turn. "(They) were neither saintly souls nor were they meddlesome busybodies. ... They were ordinary young women who felt strongly that they wanted to have a role in the great drama that was the Civil War. ... They did not always understand the culture that they entered in the South, but at the same time, they were really exceptional for their day."(5)

Not every aspect of life in St. Helena was difficult or trying. Charlotte would never forget the day she met Harriet Tubman herself. "We spent nearly all our time (with Tubman). My eyes were full as I listened to her – the heroic woman." But Charlotte spent most of her time under stress; her health was poor throughout her stay. She was an intellectual woman with no one to talk to, and she was lonely. Frail, ill and tired, she left St. Helena after only two years.

Charlotte continued to educate, but only from afar. She wrote a book on life in the South Carolina community in which she'd taught. Her book opened the eyes of those who had believed, erroneously, that former slaves could not be taught to read and write. She eventually settled in Washington, D.C., and became well-known in those intellectual circles. She eventually married a minister, Francis Grimke. Like her aunts and mother, she continued to work for equal rights and social justice. She may have been too sensitive to live the life of a teacher; that job would be left to tougher women, like Mary Ann Shadd Cary, Mary McLeod Bethune and Lucy Craft Laney. But Charlotte did embody the intellectual life of a black woman of her day. And her writings, particularly her diaries, give great insight into the world in which she lived: the affluent, educated black community that like their poorer counterparts yearned for freedom and a better life.

Lucy Craft Laney
1854-1933

If our people are going to be raised up it will be by their own bootstraps. And the bootstraps had better be strong.

Lucy Craft Laney was a single-minded woman with a single purpose: her school, Haines Normal and Industrial Institute. She would keep it open against all odds and with little help, although at least one other famous name would come passing through it: Mary McLeod Bethune.

Lucy and Mary, oddly enough, had one thing in common: their hometown. Mary was born in Mayesville, South Carolina, and Lucy's father, at least, David Laney, came from there as well. David was a former slave who had bought his freedom and preached the gospel as an Presbyterian minister. David had once been a carpenter on a large plantation near Mayesville, but after becoming a free man he moved to Macon, Georgia. There he married a slave whose freedom he bought, and the couple had two children. Lucy's mother continued to work for her former owners, the Campbells, who kindly looked the other way when young Lucy explored their home library and slowly learned to read and write.

When the Civil War ended David Laney rang the bells of Washington Avenue Presbyterian Church in celebration. Soon he and other black parents would have even more to celebrate: the Freedman's Bureau and the American Missionary Association founded a high school for blacks in Macon. As soon as an elementary school opened up, Lucy was allowed to go. When she was 15 Lucy was accepted at a well-thought-of Atlanta school. Later, that school would become the core of what is now Atlanta University. She was a member of the school's first graduating class, graduating at the top of that class, in 1873.

Lucy, now 19, went home to teach first in Macon, then Conyers, Georgia and finally in Savannah. All of these schools were held out of makeshift buildings – a church, a barn, a log cabin. The children all learned in one classroom and none of the teachers earned more than $18 a month. And none of the children would be allowed to go past the seventh grade. These schools were an improvement over what the South used to be; the illiteracy rate among Southern blacks had been as high as 90 percent at one time. After the Emancipation proclamation illiteracy had dipped to 60 percent. But to Lucy, this improvement was still not enough. Black children needed to learn about history, painting, music and literature if they were to attend black colleges like Fisk, Oberlin and Howard. Most black schools at that time, including the school run by Booker T. Washington in Tuskegee, Alabama, provided more practical education; they did not see their students going on to college.

Lucy Craft Laney felt differently, however. Since her father was a Presbyterian minister, she wrote to the Presbyterian Board of Missions to ask for help in founding a school. Her school would provide the equivalent of a high school education and live-in quarters for students and teachers. Church officials were impressed with her plans but offered no money.

Undaunted, she decided to go forth on her own. With her father's support, and one hundred dollars collected by the Ladies Aid Society of his church, Lucy moved to Augusta, Georgia in 1886.

Lucy had chosen Augusta for a reason: there were no black schools at all in that town. Augusta's Christ Presbyterian Church liked her plans enough to let her use the church basement for her class. In the beginning there was just herself and six children, but in time, more than two hundred students would crowd into her classroom.

Lucy envisioned the future Haines Institute as a boarding school for girls and a training school for teachers. But from the beginning she admitted boys, if only because she was too tender-hearted to turn them away. Her basement classroom became overcrowded within a month, forcing Lucy to rent a house from the president of the Augusta Board of Education and move the school there.

By the end of 1886 she had 75 students. By the end of 1887 she had 362 and had to rent a two-story house with a barn to house them all. Most black schools in the south combined traditional arts and science classes with job training programs because young blacks were expected to get out in the working world as soon as possible. Lucy's school was no different, but still, she wanted more for her students. She wanted to expand her curriculum as well as her classroom space. To achieve those goals, she knew she needed money. In the post-Civil War South, such money usually came from a church.

Lucy scraped up enough money for a train ticket and traveled to Minneapolis so she could talk to the Presbyterian General Assembly in person. She got no money, but she did get moral support, from Francine E.H. Haines, president of the Presbyterian Church's Woman's Department. When she came home empty-handed Lucy turned to local support, which thankfully was forthcoming. Augustans were generous, but not enough that Lucy could draw a salary. Fortunately for her, the parents of her students provided enough food so she could eat regularly.

Lucy was the only teacher at her school, in addition to being its sole administrator, and she often worked around the clock to make sure everything was done properly. She continued to attract students even though her rental agreements were tenuous and she often had to move to accommodate the growing student body. Then, in 1889, with the help of Francine Haines, the Presbyterian Board purchased a permanent site for her and put up the school's first new building,

Marshall Hall. Lucy christened her school the Haines Normal and Industrial Institute in her friend's honor.

Lucy put all these resources to good use. Her students studied the classics, Latin and Algebra and still had time for job-training. Lucy wanted her students to be able to compete in the white world, thus they had to study the kinds of subjects white children studied. And, she never missed an opportunity to build bridges between her kids and the Augusta community.

Augusta community had already built a reputation as a resort area for white Northerners, and during the winter, when such northerners were most likely to visit, Lucy did what she could to interest them in her school. The school's main "tourist" attraction, at least where whites were concerned, was its talented choir. Lucy had had a beautiful singing voice herself and now, as headmistress of her own school, oversaw the choir herself. Her music students were always on call when a visitor was on the grounds. Lucy would give the signal for them to line up and give an impromptu concert that, hopefully, would please the visitor enough that he or she would give a donation. Her concerts usually successful enough that she would get enough money to buy library books or supplement the building fund.

Over a period of several years Lucy created a strong academic program and a well-equipped kindergarten. In time she would lend her support to the creation of a new city hospital and found a training program for nurses out of her school. By the time Lucy accepted the application of a young teacher, Mary McLeod Bethune, to join her staff Haines Normal and Industrial Institute had grown to include a three-story building and several residential cottages. Lucy's was a well-ordered school: a large library, art classes, that well-trained and well-regarded choir and a large student body. Bethune, a future mover and shaker in her own right, would fondly remember her days with Lucy. She looked to Lucy as her mentor and inspiration for future endeavors. More than anything else, Lucy's school gave hope to those who might not be able to make their way otherwise. "Her school was a torchlight in the community," Mary would remember. "Still there were hundreds and hundreds of people who were not touched. I roomed on the third floor, and I could look out of my windows into the alleyways of (the neighborhood) and see masses of unkempt children, just trying to find their way as best they could."(1)

Lucy Craft Laney would never marry: her life was given over to education. When she died, in 1933, she was buried on the grounds of her school, fittingly enough. However, just a few years after her death the Presbyterian Church withdrew its financial support: the toll from the Great Depression had simply been too much. Lucy's friends and supporters were able to keep it going for a while, but finally, in 1949, Haines Normal closed. Yet Lucy Craft Laney's legacy lived on and she had received many honors before an after her death. She is one of three black Georgia residents whose portrait hangs in the state capitol. The city of Augusta renamed Gwinnett Street, where the school was located, Laney-Walker Boulevard in her honor: the name also honors Charles T. Walker, co-founder of Atlanta University. Lucy's Augusta home was restored in 1991 and opened to the public as the Lucy Craft Laney Museum of Black History.

(Photo courtesy of the Museum in Memory of Virginia E. Randolph)

Virginia Estelle Randolph
(1874-1958)

There is no need for a mind if you can't use your hands.

Virginia Estelle Randolph followed a different drummer throughout her life. She came of age as a teacher in a time when most black educators clamored for a new emphasis on academics. Black children needed to study literature, mathematics and languages, not learn how to work. Virginia believed that while young blacks should indeed study reading and writing, they would be better off learning job skills as well. This idea was out of fashion by the time Virginia entered teaching, yet she would pursue it zealously until the end of her career.

Virginia was born in Richmond, Virginia, in 1874 to Sarah Elizabeth Carter and Edward Nelson Randolph, both of whom were former slaves. Sarah had remained friendly enough with her former owner, a professor at Old Richmond College,that he witnessed her marriage to Edward for her and suggested names for her children.

Sarah was widowed young and suffered through the same struggles that any single mother experiences. She brought up her children in a tiny home and worked day and night, as a domestic, so she could feed and clothe them. To make matters worse, after the Civil WarVirginia was not an easy place for blacks. Reconstruction was going on, white southerners were resentful, and things could be trying both economically and politically.

Yet schools for black children did exist and Virginia would enter one at the age of six. She received a medal for highest honors at the end of her first term, and 10 years later, at the age of 16, she passed her teaching exam with flying colors.

Although certified, Virginia was considered too young to teach. One of her relatives lent a hand and got her got a job teaching school in Goochland County, Virginia. Two years later, she took on a far more challenging assignment. At the age of 18, Virginia would run a one-room school in Henrico County, Virginia.

The school was known as Mountain Road School and it was badly in need of repair and refurbishment. Virginia sought help from the community and returned what she got ten-fold. She visited adults throughout the county regularly, teaching them health care, nutrition, homemaking and needlework. The education she offered her students was every bit as practical. Perhaps owing to the struggles she'd seen her mother go through, Virginia firmly believed in the all-around development of the child. She taught girls to garden and cook and sew and boys how to make handicrafts from honeysuckle vines and hickory and work with wood. She even went so far as to dismantle a neighbor's stove one day while it was still warm and take it to school so she could teach a cooking class. Undoubtedly influenced by another advocate of "practical" education, Booker T. Washington, Virginia taught manual skills as well as religion and morality in her school.

Her classes, and techniques, sparked controversy from the very beginning. Some Mountain Road parents protested: they wanted their children learning mathematics and composition, not gardening, they said. At one point they even circulated a petition to have Virginia removed. But the Henrico County school superintendent stood by her in the end, and in time, Virginia would gain an important ally from outside the state of Virginia.

In 1907, Anna Jeanes, a Quaker woman who'd inherited a great deal of money and wanted to put it to good use, founded the Negro Rural School Fund, a project meant to improve small rural schools for southern blacks. The fund attracted some famous trustees: Booker T. Washington, industrialist and philanthropist Andrew Carnegie, Robert Moton and James Dillard. The Jeanes Fund, as it became known, employed hundreds of black teachers, via grants, in the first decades of the 20th century. The very first of them to supervise industrial education was Virginia Randolph.

Virginia received her Jeanes grant thanks to a man named Jackson Davis: he was the same Henrico County school superintendent who'd backed her up in the face of such strong parental disapproval. Davis, like Virginia, believed in industrial education and job training for young blacks, particularly after he visited the school founded by Booker T. Washington. Davis wanted black industrial education in Henrico County, but had been denied county funding to implement what proved to be an unpopular idea. But the Jeanes grant gave him leeway: he had visited Virginia's school and was impressed with her teaching methods. Her work could do a lot of good, he believed. Teachers throughout the state needed supervision and training in her methods, and black adults needed outside help to improve their nutrition, health care and hygiene. With help from the Jeanes grant, Virginia could make this happen, he felt.

Virginia would devote the rest of her career to training teachers and developing community outreach. The same year she became a Jeanes teacher she organized a community effort that was a prototype for her lifelong concern. On March 30, 1908, she conducted the first ever Arbor Day celebration in the state of Virginia. Putting her students to work, she planted 12 sycamore trees, named for the 12 disciples of Jesus, on the grounds of Mountain Road school.

Virginia became a Jeanes teacher when she was 34 years old. She was in charge of assisting and directing county teachers in their efforts to help the black community. Thanks to the grant money she now had the freedom to shape industrial training and community self-help programs the way she wanted. In time she would supervise programs in 23 schools. And in its quiet way, Virginia's work was truly ground-breaking. It would be the first formal, in-service teacher training for rural black teachers offered anywhere in the country. And thanks to her efforts, the quality of education in Virginia's rural, one-room schools improved. The school term was lengthened, student attendance improved, school buildings were better maintained and county training schools for teachers were introduced. Virginia accomplished all these things at a time when southern schools remained segregated and black students often suffered under the "separate but equal" principle of education.

Virginia painstakingly recorded her accomplishments. She listed improvements made at each of the schools under her care. Her program became known as "the Henrico Plan." Her reports were reprinted and sent to superintendents throughout the South, and her teaching techniques were adopted as far away as Africa.

Virginia's work included a lot of travel but she adapted to this gamely. A newspaper account of her work published this description of the troubles she faced on the road: "To reach the 23 schools she supervised, trips that took up to three hours one way on muddy country roads, Randolph had to hire a buggy and driver, an expense that consumed much of her salary. Later she bought her own horse."(1)

Her salary and expenses were also eaten up by another concern: the many children she took in over the years. She never married or had a family of her own, but the children of Henrico County, especially those old enough to attend Mountain Road School, were her concern. At any given time Virginia might have a dozen children living with her in her home. This free "board" had a practical bent: the children of Mountain Road had no school buses to ride and some lived too far away to walk. Virginia would shelter them in her home so they could attend classes during the school year. Later in life she even bought a private bus for them, so they could ride back and forth from home to school. During her lifetime, Virginia helped, and gave shelter to, roughly 59 children.

Virginia continued to press for a black high school to be built in Henrico County. She got her wish in 1915, when the Virginia Randolph Training School opened. Virginia went on to raise money to build boys and girls dormitories at the school. She became so wrapped up in this new project that when it accidentally burnt to the ground in 1929, she had to be put under a doctor's care temporarily.

But the school was later rebuilt, even bigger and better. Virginia went back to work and until she finally retired, 20 years later. She had had a long and productive career as an educator, social worker and humanitarian. She had served her home state of Virginia for 57 years.

Before she left teaching Virginia was given the William E. Harmon Award for Distinguished Achievement. She would be the first black American, man or woman, to be so honored. After her retirement, a Virginia Estelle Randolph fund was established to assist boys and girls who attended southern rural schools.

A museum in Virginia's memory was dedicated in 1970. Six years later, the Virginia Randolph Home Economics Cottage museum was named a national historic landmark by the United States Department of Interior, National Park Service. It is located on the campus of the Virginia Randolph Education complex, 2200 Mountain Road, Glen Allen, Virginia, and visitors can tour the museum free of charge, among its collections are Virginia Randolph's personal possessions and the photographs she took during her career. And the original Sycamore trees she and her students planted are still growing on the grounds. They have been named Notable, or historic, trees of Virginia, and they are part of the living legacy of Virginia Randolph.

Notes

Maria Louise Baldwin

1. Hallie Q. Brown, *Homespun Heroines and Other Women of Distinction.* 1988: Oxford University Press, N.Y., Page 185.

2. Charles W. Wadelington and Richard F. Knapp, *Charlotte Hawkins Brown and Palmer Memorial Institute.* University of North Carolina Press, Chapel Hill & London, 1999, Page 30.

3. "Maria L. Baldwin School," www.cps.ci.cambridge.ma .us/element/Baldwin/

4. "Maria L. Baldwin School," www.cps.ci.cambridge.ma .us/element/Baldwin/

5. Darryl Lyman. *Great African American Women.* Gramercy Books, NY 1999, Page 16.

6. "Maria L. Baldwin School," www.cps.ci.cambridge.ma .us/element/Baldwin/

7. Darryl Lyman. *Great African American Women*, Page 16.

8. Nathaniel Vogel, "The Mismeasure of Maria Baldwin," www.afsc.org/pwork, page 2.

Mary McLeod Bethune

1. Emma Gelders Sterne. *Mary McLeod Bethune*, Page 70.

2. Catherine Owens Peare. *Mary McLeod Bethune*. The Vanguard Press, New York, 1951, Page 73

3. Emma Gelders Sterne. *Mary McLeod Bethune*, Page 190.

4. Emma Gelders Sterne. *Mary McLeod Bethune*, Page 203.

5. Emma Gelders Sterne. *Mary McLeod Bethune*, Page 214.

6. Robert A. Caro, *The Years of Lyndon Johnson, Master of the Senate*, 2002: Alfred A. Knopf, New York, Page 729.

Charlotte Hawkins Brown

1. Charles W. Wadelington and Richard F. Knapp,. *Charlotte Hawkins Brown and Palmer Memorial Institute.* University of North Carolina Press, Chapel Hill & London, 1999, Page 30.

2. Charles W. Wadelington and Richard F. Knapp,. *Charlotte Hawkins Brown and Palmer Memorial Institute,* Page 91

3. Tonya Bolden, *The Book of African-American Women*, Adams Media Corporation, Holbrook, Massachusetts, 1996, Page 127.

Mary Shadd Cary

1. Jane Rhodes. *Mary Ann Shadd Cary, The Black Press and Protest in the Nineteenth Century.* 1998: Indiana University Press, Bloomington, Page 21.

2. Jane Rhodes. *Mary Ann Shadd Cary, The Black Press and Protest in the Nineteenth Century*, Page 38.

3. Jane Rhodes. *Mary Ann Shadd Cary, The Black Press and Protest in the Nineteenth Century*, Page 127.

4. Jane Rhodes. *Mary Ann Shadd Cary, The Black Press and Protest in the Nineteenth Century*, Page 171.

5. Jane Rhodes. *Mary Ann Shadd Cary, The Black Press and Protest in the Nineteenth Century*, Page 155.

6. Jane Rhodes. *Mary Ann Shadd Cary, The Black Press and Protest in the Nineteenth Century* Page 202.

Marva Collins

1.Marva Collins and Civia Tamarkin, "Marva Collins' Way," J.P. Tarcher Inc., Los Angeles, Page 212.

2. Marva Collins and Civia Tamarkin, "Marva Collins' Way," Page 41.

3. Marva Collins and Civia Tamarkin, "Marva Collins' Way," Page 43

4. Marva Collins and Civia Tamarkin, "Marva Collins' Way," Page 45.

5. Marva Collins and Civia Tamarkin, "Marva Collins' Way," Page 110

6. Marva Collins and Civia Tamarkin, "Marva Collins' Way," Page 140

7. Marva Collins and Civia Tamarkin, "Marva Collins' Way," Page 141

Charlotte Forten Grimke

1. "PBS Online: Only a Teacher: Schoolhouse Pioneers, Charlotte Forten Grimke, www.pbs.org/onlyateacher/charlotte.

2. Nancy Hoffman. *"Women's True Profession, Voices from the History of Teaching,"* The Feminist Press, Old Westbury, New York, 1981, page 155

3. Nancy Hoffman. *"Women's True Profession, Voices from the History of Teaching,"* Page 149.

4. "PBS Online: Only a Teacher: Schoolhouse Pioneers, Charlotte Forten Grimke, www.pbs.org/onlyateacher/charlotte.

5. "PBS Online: Only a Teacher: Schoolhouse Pioneers, Charlotte Forten Grimke, www.pbs.org/onlyateacher/charlotte.

Lucy Craft Laney

1. Catherine Owens Peare. *Mary McLeod Bethune.* The Vanguard Press, New York, 1951, Page 76.

Virginia Estelle Randolph.

1. Robin Farmer. "Virginia Randolph," Richmond Times-Dispatch, Richmond, VA Feb. 17, 2003.

Bibliography

BOOKS

Tonya Bolden, *The Book of African-American Women*, 1996: Adams Media Corporation, Holbrook, Massachusetts, .

Hallie Q. Brown, *Homespun Heroines and Other Women of Distinction.* 1988: Oxford University Press, N.Y.

Robert A. Caro, *The Years of Lyndon Johnson, Master of the Senate*, 2002: Alfred A. Knopf, New York.

Marva Collins, Cynthia Tamarkin. *Marva Collins' Way*, 1982: J.P. Tarcher, Inc., Los Angeles, CA.

Emma Gelders Sterne. *Mary McLeod Bethune.* Alfred A. Knopf, New York, 1957.

Darlene Clark Hine, ed. *Facts on File Encyclopedia*

of Black Women in America, Facts on File, Inc., New York, 1997.

Nancy Hoffman. *"Women's True Profession, Voices from the History of Teaching,"* The Feminist Press, Old Westbury, New York, 1981.

Darryl Lyman. *Great African American Women*, Gramercy Books, NY 1999.

Catherine Owens Peare. *Mary McLeod Bethune*, The Vanguard Press, New York, 1951.

Jane Rhodes. *Mary Ann Shadd Cary, The Black Press and Protest in the Nineteenth Century*. 1998: Indiana University Press, Bloomington, Indiana.

Charles W. Wadelington and Richard F. Knapp, *Charlotte Hawkins Brown and Palmer Memorial Institute*. University of North Carolina Press, Chapel Hill & London, 1999

Mary Wilds. *Mumbet, the Life and Times of Elizabeth Freeman*, 1999: Avisson Press, Greensboro, North Carolina.

PERIODICALS

Jerry Adler and Donna Foote. "The Marva Collins Story," *Newsweek*, March 8, 1982.

Robin Farmer. "Virginia Randolph," *Richmond Times-Dispatch*, Richmond, VA Feb. 17, 2003.

Dan Hurley. "The Teacher Who Broke the Rules," *50 Plus*, June, 1986.

Joy Bennett Kinnon. "Marva Collins: The Collins Creed," *Ebony*, December, 1996.

Marilyn Marshall. "Marva Collins: Educator Weathers the Storm," *Ebony*, February, 1985.

INTERNET SOURCES

"Maria Baldwin-A Woman of Education: Black History Daily," *www.blackseek.com*.

"Maria Louise Baldwin," *www.africanpubs.com*

"Maria L. Baldwin School,"
www.cps.ci.cambridge.ma .us/element/Baldwin/

"Georgia Women of Achievement: 1992 Inductee
Lucy Craft Laney,"
*www.mindspring.com/~gwa/honorees/long/laney1_*
long.htm.

"Lucy Craft Laney,"
www.lucycraftlaneymuseum.com

"PBS Online: Only a Teacher: Schoolhouse
pioneers, Charlotte Forten Grimke,"
www.pbs.org/onlyateacher/charlotte.

Nathaniel Vogel, "The Mismeasure of Maria
Baldwin," *www.afsc.org/pwork*

Index

About the Author

MARY WILDS is the author of several books for Young Adults. Among them are *Mumbet,* a slave narrative, and *Raggin' the Blues,* portraits of legendary blues and ragtime musicians.